Understanding Management Accounting

SECOND EDITION

by

T. M. WALKER, CA, ACMA

Senior Lecturer in Management Accounting,
The Institute of Chartered Accountants of Scotland

GEE & CO (PUBLISHERS) LIMITED
151 STRAND, LONDON WC2R 1JJ

FIRST EDITION 1979
SECOND EDITION 1982
© GEE & CO (PUBLISHERS) LIMITED
ISBN 085258 226 9

Printed in Great Britain by Staples Printers St Albans Limited at The Priory Press, Hertfordshire

Contents

Introduction

The scope of this publication is not intended to be exhaustive; the purpose of the author is to 'disarm' many of the disagreeable problems which students of management accounting too often find at dangerously late stages of their studies. They may then, through a lack of lucid and palatable text-books which really *explain* matters, find themselves unsure of the vital principles and reasons behind the techniques.

As far as can be gleaned from reports issued by inscrutable examiners, there is a greater need than ever for today's management accounting candidates to be able to interpret with skill and acumen the figure-work performance reports which they themselves prepare, or which are offered within question texts. Such narrative expertise will be greatly assisted by the lucid commentary presented by the author. He concerns himself not only with 'how' to apply management accounting techniques, but 'why' commerce and industry hold them in high regard. In his observations on the purposes, caveats and advantages of utilising certain management accounting skills, without belabouring detail, the author is filling a text-book vacuum which has been created by too much attention to the preparation of figure-work examples without sufficient explanation.

The style is very readable and should appeal to a wide variety of readers. In particular, those who have recently entered or are about to enter the variegated landscapes of a more detailed course, whether on a block-release, day-release, evening class, correspondence or other basis should find the book of immense help in clarifying the doubts and uncertainties which arise when students are plunged into detailed problems without sufficient time to build strong foundations of understanding. In particular, detailed knowledge of individual segments of management accounting is often accumulated without a good grounding in how these parts knit together. Those in industry and commerce who wish to be reminded in rapid fashion of key issues concerning salient areas of management accounting should find this book of benefit.

The author, a qualified Chartered Accountant and Cost and Management Accountant, spent a number of years in a large professional firm after qualifying, and then moved into industry where, for eight years, he held management positions within the accounting functions of three large international groups of companies. He is presently Senior Lecturer in Management Accounting at The Institute of Chartered Accountants of Scotland, a position which he has held since 1973. He has also been the Examiner in Management Accounting and Business Finance at The Institute of Bankers in Scotland since 1974.

Acknowledgments

I am indebted to The Institute of Bankers in Scotland for allowing me to draw on and expand in this publication parts of a Study Guide which I prepared for the Institute's Management Accounting and Business Finance candidates. I am grateful also to The Institute of Chartered Accountants of Scotland for allowing the use of portions of narrative which first appeared as documentation for students, and to Mrs Rona Johnston and Mrs Irene McKain for their highly proficient secretarial and typing work.

1 Cost Control and Absorption

There can be no doubt that cost control is one of the essential strands in the pattern of management accounting; but for practical managers and students of the subject alike, cost control has the aura of a police action. Those directly involved apply or recoil from disciplinary procedures according to relative positions on organisational charts. The aspects of cost control which are both positive and interesting too often lie buried beneath a company's routine efforts to compare actual and budgeted costs and show differences between the two.

The positive side of cost control is not founded on an attempt to impose moderation and restraint upon cavalier employees: it is based on the principle that actual expenditure should not exceed what ultimate actual end products are capable of carrying to market. Thus the unbudgeted champagne bottle can be broken open when the unbudgeted sales order has been captured. The cost budget is not the ultimate resting place for the bill: only the penultimate. The final home for the bill will be a customer's invoice.

Monitoring System

Those who operate cost control procedures, therefore, must monitor increases and decreases in the levels of saleable activity. To over-simplify, an increase in spending of 60% can be a cause for celebration if saleable production is up by 80%. The cost controller must have a sound knowledge of the entire canvas of operations to enable him to prompt the correct responses to expenditure from his colleagues. He must assess planned and actual expenditure against two criteria:

(1) there must be a product which can carry the *type* of expense in question in terms of common justice and relevancy:
(2) the *amount* of the expense should be capable of standing scrutiny by customers in the clear light of day, having regard to product quality and quantity.

Such championing of potential customers in the market place begins well in advance of production and selling activity: this is the saving feature of good cost control. The preparation of budgets involves management in anticipation of the reactions of knowledgeable and discerning customers and there can be rather too much crystal-ball gazing for comfort. A supplier's spending acceleration rate can outpace the rate of growth of his customer's willingness to re-pay: and the longer the delay between spending by a supplier and recovery from a customer, the greater the need for cost control by the former, particularly if, for a proportion of this time lag, the customer remains uncommitted and the goods or services remain in stock.

Cost control should include analyses of product, process or job costs into elements such as direct labour, direct material, power and depreciation so that each element is expressed as a percentage of total cost, at both the planned and actual stages. In this way impending pressure points can be identified which might otherwise cause trading difficulties: for example, if an escalation in the price of fuel oil is foreseen, knowledge of whether fuel oil represents 5% or 35% of finished product cost will be vital in planning future actions such as a change to another type of fuel or implementation of price-volume relationship studies.

Cost control (therefore) involves (a) before the event anticipation of (or budgeting for) saleable activity levels and consequent relevant and sustainable expenditure, (b) collection of actual expenditure, (c) measurement of actual activity levels, (d) revision of cost entitlement in view of actual activity levels and finally (e) a constructive comparison between actual costs and the budgeted costs for both actual and budgeted activity levels.

While each of the above segments of cost control is often regarded as a separate topic in its own right, I have tended to regard them as a single package within this text, in that they all lead to the ultimate acid test: will a customer pay?

7

COST CONTROL PROCEDURES

If responsibility for cost control can be attributed to specific managers, explanations on variances between actual and budgeted costs can usually emanate from the same individuals. The cornerstone of cost control is comparison of actual with planned (or expected) costs, and the investigation of differences between the two by pre-determined managers.

Every cost incurred by an organisation should be controlled: this is done by charging it via a prime document such as an invoice, a stores requisition or an employee's time sheet to the point of origin of that cost. For this purpose the point of origin is defined as a 'cost centre' or 'cost collection centre'. A cost centre may be a very small fragment indeed, perhaps a single machine (either for manufacturing or, say, for photocopying), or a group of machines. Within each cost centre there should be some key business resource which generates ACTIVITY, either saleable activity such as the painting of motor cars, or some internal service activity such as the generation of steam power to activate production machinery or the cooking of meals for company employees. Where a key business resource is found to exist, with some measurable objective as described above, other supporting resources tend to accumulate in support, so that a group of resources becomes bound together in the fulfilment of certain definable tasks. The pursuit of these objectives provokes costs or causes costs to happen. When costs occur, they are charged to this point of origin so that they may be COMPARED with expected costs. The latter must be FLEXED (or adjusted) into line with actual ACTIVITY, when budgeted and actual activity differ, so that like can be compared with like. The controlling of every cost incurred through a cost centre ensures that the making of profits by an organisation is coupled with careful use of its resources, because in the final reckoning profit is measured against capital employed, and on this assessment management performance is judged.

Dangers of Overspending

Budgeted costs normally form the basis for quoting to customers and for pricing policy. Consequently overspending can result in certain costs being non-recoverable; conversely, if actual costs fall below expectations, prices quoted may be overstated with the result that orders may be lost to competitors. There is always a very real threat that adverse spending variances constitute 'lost cash' and that cost savings may not be passed on to the sales and marketing departments quickly enough to capture or hold customers. In addition, budgeted costs form the basis for negotiations with banks on the timing and extent of overdrafts. In severe cases, therefore, overspending which is not discovered quickly and rectified in time can cause acute liquidity problems.

Creating a Cost Centre Reporting System

Undernoted are some of the ground rules which should apply when a cost centre reporting system is being established:

(1) Responsibility for cost control within a particular cost centre should be clearly defined. There should be one manager who is answerable for direct costs charged to any particular centre and to whom a comparison of actual and budgeted costs will prove helpful.

(2) There should be a clear distinction within the reporting format between those costs capable of direct allocation and control, and those charged to a centre on a re-apportionment basis after initial control elsewhere.

(3) While it may be reasonably straightforward to attempt to budget cost levels within a particular cost centre, and to lay out these forecasts in good order on reports, great care must be taken to ensure that actual costs in due course are effectively analysed to the same level of detail as shown in budgets and to the same 'points of origin' (cost centres) as have calculated budgeted costs. To this end, accounting codes are normally employed, and adequate staff training is essential to ensure that these are understood.

(4) For the purposes of interpretation of results and effective control of costs, both budgeted and actual costs within a cost centre are analysed by expense classification (or element of cost); the most common are wages, salaries, materials, and power. Expense classifications should all be clearly defined to avoid ambiguity, which in turn can cause many differences between actual and budgeted expense. Problems of comparison arise when a budgeted cost is reported under one expense classification, and the actual cost for the item concerned is coded and duly charged to another expense classification. Two expense lines on the cost centre report are then affected, one showing a variance of actual above budget, the other a variance through actual being below budget.

(5) Budgeted and actual costs should be arranged together for easy comparison. Differences between the two, normally known as variances, should appear in a separate column.

(6) Expense classifications within a cost centre report should be arranged in a logical sequence, with direct expenses, directly attributable to that cost centre at the top of the page, followed by apportionments of expenses, charged out firstly from other 'close' cost centres which tend to be located under the same roof, eg from service departments for heating and lighting, canteen, printing and stationery, etc, and secondly from the more 'remote' cost centres, eg re-apportionments of expense from regional or head offices; finally, controlled cost leaving the cost centre concerned and being charged out to other cost centres should be shown, analysed by destination: many service department cost centres, after controlling their own direct costs and indeed accumulating apportionments of cost from other cost centres, pass on their entire costs to other cost centres, in particular to manufacturing cost centres which tend to act as assembly points for all costs which are incurred in bringing saleable produce to a location and condition in which it can be deemed finished (or ready).

Expense Classification Lists

It is common for organisations to issue standardised code lists covering their expense classifications. Thus, whether a manager be responsible for steel production, distribution, or personnel work, his cost centre report is likely to be analysed by common elements of cost which have standard definitions throughout that organisation. Some of the advantages of standardised expense classifications appear below.

(1) Summarisation of classifications of cost is facilitated. This may involve arriving at a total of a particular cost, say, salaries, for an entire group of companies, or for a single company, or for a division, an area, or a particular function of that company eg selling.

(2) In the wake of standardisation of expense classifications, clear definitions are normally issued, and the introduction of a manual of account codes is facilitated. Consequently differences between actual and budgeted expense are much less likely to be caused by ambiguities in terminology, resulting in budgeted expense going to one expense classification, and actual to another.

(3) Comparisons between cost centres, locations, companies etc are facilitated. For example, salesmen's travel expenses on the business of one division of a company may be compared with those of the salesmen of another division, if the meaning of 'travelling expenses' is common to both divisions.

(4) Comparison between accounting periods, and, within a period, between actual and budgeted expense is facilitated when the coding of particular items is not subject to variations through ambiguity or lack of precise definition.

(5) Inter-staff mobility and communications are eased.

(6) Pre-printing of accounting forms, either as regards narrative content or particular routine codes becomes possible.

(7) Training can be undertaken on a central basis, ie through issue of a standard instructional

manual, covering the needs of staff engaged in all the areas in which the common expense classifications are in use.

(8) Economic computer-based cost control systems are facilitated. In many cases, only one master file of expense classifications need be maintained, for storing narrative descriptions of expense classifications for printing purposes. There may then be no need to build in a check-routine as to which segment of the total organisation is using an expense class code, which under non-standardised conditions, would be necessary when a particular code would have a different meaning to each segment.

Creating Cost Centres

Whether a particular cost centre has been chosen wisely can be decided by a few tests, some of which are listed below:

(1) It should be possible in due course to directly attribute the actual equivalents to budgeted costs to a particular centre if they are to be directly controlled there. Salary costs may provide a case in point, when certain employees may have responsibilities stretching across cost centre frontiers which are loosely defined. Arbitrary splitting of major costs such as salaries weakens the effectiveness of cost accumulation for decision making.

(2) Ideally the resources (manpower, machinery etc) within a cost centre should be clearly defined in advance. Each cost centre, if properly crystalised, should be capable of performing some measurable task(s) which have clear definition and are spelled out in objectives to be met in each accounting period. Apparent over-spending evidenced by adverse variances between actual and budgeted costs, could be beneficial if additional objectives have been met.

(3) The close association of each cost centre to a particular manager should facilitate forward planning of anticipated activity and consequent cost levels. For example, a recruitment officer, undecided as to whether to go on a 'milk round' of schools or universities to interview potential trainees, would be required to finalise his plans in order to complete his budgeted costs under the expense classification of, say, 'Travel'. Again, a training officer, postponing a decision on hiring an overhead projector for training purposes, would need to make up his mind before completing his estimate of 'Equipment Hire'. A branch manager in banking circles would need to discuss academic training plans with his staff before finalising 'Training course and exam fees', and so on.

(4) In particular, a cost centre draws together a certain mix of resources, and measures expenditure in the light of what these resources achieve in a given period.

Production Cost Centres

The characteristics of a manufacturing or production cost centre include the following:

(1) Measurable, tangible value should be added within a manufacturing cost centre to a saleable product. Where the task of inspection is performed in a separate, autonomous department, such a cost centre cannot be classed as manufacturing. Inspection merely checks that the value added by manufacturing cost centres is sustainable in the books of account, ie in line with the evidence of the actual physical condition of the products concerned. Similarly a tool repair shop certainly exists for the general well-being of production, but the cost centres which requisition tools from the tool shop and apply them to specific products which pass through on their way to completion come under the banner of manufacturing cost centres, and not the tool shop itself, (unless, of course, tools are made for direct sale to third party customers).

(2) Product input to and output from a manufacturing cost centre should be clearly definable and capable of measurement, ie the amount and value of saleable commodity, such as

unpainted toy buses being transferred into a department, and painted buses being transferred out, must be measureable.

(3)   Key resources earmarked to a particular cost centre, eg manpower and machinery, floor space, materials etc should be defined and clearly identifiable.
(4)   There should be stability of boundaries so that performance targets can be set.
(5)   Responsibilities for performance should be attributed to specific persons.

Service Cost Centres

Many of the characteristics of a manufacturing cost centre are also attributable to a service cost centre. However the latter do not directly handle saleable commodities in the sense of adding any tangible value. For example, distributed (or transported) goods will (hopefully) look much the same as undistributed goods (apart from occasional dents on packaging) so that the distribution cost centre is classed as a service cost centre. Similarly, canteen, first aid, personnel, powerhouse and engineering are regarded as service department cost centres.

Direct Charges to Cost Centres

Every cost incurred should be charged or debited to some cost centre or other for the purposes of control. These direct charges are so-called when there is no intermediate or intervening cost centre between the cash book or purchase day book (or other book or original entry) and the cost centre which is achieving the control. This means that the expense levels incurred are controlled and that responsibility for specific differences between actual and budgeted expense levels is pinned down to particular individuals. Thus a cost centre receiving a direct charge of expense becomes a 'cost object' with a particular purpose ie of cost control in mind.

Collecting Costs at Different Levels

In management accounting there are many different kinds of cost object to which costs may be attached; each has its own particular uses when it comes to management decision making. Products (or product groups) are well known types of cost object. A particular location of an organisation may be another cost object for another level of decision making. For example, a particular branch of a bank may be under appraisal and the running costs may be directed or attached to the branch. Again, a particular machine, perhaps a computer, can become a cost object at various times if decisions are necessary in the processing field.

When a management accounting system is being installed it is important that (a) *routine* cost objects are wisely chosen for maximum decision-making potential and (b) a good proportion of costs incurred can be *directly* attributed and charged to those cost objects. The system is then geared to attach costs to the regular, pre-determined cost objects on a day-to-day basis, rather than on an ad-hoc, once-off basis, the latter being much more expensive in time and effort.

Distinguishing Direct and Indirect Costs

'Indirect' costs are those which find their way to a particular cost object via an intermediate stop. For example, the heating expense of a particular office cost centre within a building may be controlled in an 'Office Services' cost centre, to which electricity bills are directly charged as a direct expense for comparison with budget. However, the Office Services cost centre may then apportion the electricity bill to other cost centres on some equitable basis. To these latter cost centres, the electricity costs are indirect expenses; certainly they have been attached to various 'customer' cost centres of Office Services, but only indirectly.

In a manufacturing environment, a foreman may work full time in manufacturing cost centre A. When analysis of the payroll takes place, his salary can safely be charged to A. However he may spend his time dealing with several product cost objects within the department, on rather a

11

random basis, without keeping time-sheet records which could be coded to particular product cost objects. When the cost of making each product is being worked out, the foreman's salary must of course be included in relevant costs, but it is an indirect expense in the sense that the cost centre has formed an intermediate stop-point (between the wages sheets in the wages office and the products concerned) to which the salary cost has first been charged, and in which an absorption rate into individual products has been calculated on some arbitrary basis.

A very high proportion of expense in industry and commerce can be *directly* charged both to particular products worked upon within a cost centre *and* to the cost centre itself. Direct materials and direct labour are major examples. In such cases the direct charge to product cost objects usually takes precedence in the sense that WORK-IN-PROGRESS account is debited or charged in the nominal (or general) ledger, and the charge to the particular cost centre concerned is made in a subsidiary ledger as a memorandum away from the double-entry book-keeping routine and trial-balance. Charges to both levels of cost-object ought to take place as a matter of routine, through effective use of accounting codes, because a wide range of helpful decisions can come from accumulation of costs both by cost-centre and by product. However, the higher the proportion of indirect cost which finds its way (eventually) to a particular cost object, via guess-work allocation or some so-called arbitrary means, the less reliable is the total accumulation of cost and the less dependable are the decisions which can be made.

Taking Decisions after Collecting Costs

The following examples illustrate why costs might be accumulated for cost centres in addition to any product cost accumulations which might take place:

(1) A decision might be needed as to whether to operate a staff canteen as an alternative to the issue of luncheon vouchers. Unless the *full* cost of the canteen can be estimated, a comparative cost statement is impossible.
(2) There might be uncertainty as to whether an internal service department for, say, maintenance and repairs would be preferable to obtaining on an ad-hoc basis the occasional services of outside contractors.
(3) Comparative costs of a company's own transport and the charges of outside hauliers might be needed to determine the more economic method of fulfilling distribution needs.

The *principal* objective served by re-apportionment of costs from one cost centre to another is to ensure that product cost objects which are eventually sold to customers are not under-priced. When a product, be it goods or services, (such as plumbing work to members of the public), is sold, the total accumulated cost of making and providing the product is naturally significant. Sales are measured against the cost of those sales in arriving at profit. Frequently organisations take comfort from the fact that in arriving at product costs, a proportion of each and every cost incurred has been included, often by apportionment of costs to manufacturing cost centres through which production passes, and at which costs can be attached by means of recovery rates. This absorption costing method spreads all manner of costs, from canteen cutlery to personnel managers' salaries across saleable products which are often extremely remote from the points of cost incurrence and control responsibility. The acid test in allowing costs to be absorbed into the costs of saleable products is whether such costs have been incurred in 'bringing stock to its present condition and location'. Consequently, decisions as to whether to treat, say, works accounting department costs as part of ultimate product costs (part of product stock valuation) are 'touch and go': if, in such a case, works accounting spent most of their time helping production management to control current production, by producing pertinent ongoing information on daily performance, then the works accounting department costs could safely be regarded as part of stock valuation.

Determining the Cost of Products

Managements of manufacturing and service organisations are concerned to build aggregate product costs:

(1) to facilitate realistic pricing policy
(2) to determine profit
(3) to ensure stock valuation in line with accounting principles.

As soon as a cost becomes a part of product costs, (ie held within Work-in-Progress, and when work is complete within Finished Goods in the Nominal or General Ledger), management have the right to withdraw that cost from current charges (debits) in the company's trading or profit and loss account, and carry the cost forward to the ensuing period, as an opening debit (or charge), PROVIDED they believe it to be realisable in ensuing periods, and provided the goods are as yet unsold.

Treatment of Product Costs

To simplify matters (greatly), a product cost will in due course be debited to Cost of Sales Account and hence to Profit and Loss Account, having been credited earlier to Bank Account thus reducing the bank balance. Hopefully, the cost will be passed on to a customer, in which case there will be a debit to Debtors and a credit to Sales and thence to the Profit and Loss Account. A product cost only reaches these ultimate stages at the time of sale: prior to that time, it is passed from period to period, never reaching the Cost of Sales Account in the ledger. Prior to time of sale, product cost in effect lies in the Balance Sheet as an asset as part of Work-in-Progress or Finished Goods stock: the Profit and Loss Account does not suffer a charge, nor does it receive a credit for any sales.

However cost which is not regarded as bringing stock to its present condition and location is in effect debited immediately to Cost of Sales of the period when incurred, and thence charged to the Profit and Loss Account, having been credited to Bank to reduce the bank balance. It is up to the management of the company to ensure appropriate pricing policies to try to recover such costs from customers.

Absorbing Overheads into Product Costs

Direct materials and direct labour are charged to specific products by means of stores requisition slips or direct coding of purchase orders or invoices in the case of direct materials, and job cards, time sheets, or wages analysis sheets in the case of direct labour (or direct wages). Any other cost which is to be regarded as product cost must first of all find its way to the manufacturing or operating cost centres where products are dealt with. This may be done (a) by direct charging to such cost centres, eg of the foreman's salary, or the lubricating oil of particular machines which belong to a specific cost centre, or computer stationery which clearly can be directly charged to one cost centre, or (b) by apportionment of a proportion of a total cost which has firstly been directly charged in some other cost centre, eg heat and light, or power, or rates.

Costs which, unlike direct materials and direct labour, cannot be directly charged to products within a cost centre, are attached to products by means of an overhead recovery rate. The normal procedure involves estimating (or budgeting) the level of production activity to be achieved in an impending period, and the consequent level of production overheads to be expected. The latter is then divided by the former to derive a production overhead recovery rate per unit of production activity.

The costs which should become part of this overhead recovery system according to best accounting practice, are those costs which are being incurred in bringing the production activity units to their present condition and location, excluding, of course, direct materials and direct labour which are directly charged through other procedures and do not become duplicated at the overhead recovery stage. As has been implied earlier, many interesting discussions have been taking place recently about which particular items should be classified as having been incurred in bringing stock to its present condition and location. Many would regard the salaries of FACTORY or WORKS management as product costs, because they are concerned with the day to day well-being of production activity and their energies tend to be expended in ongoing routine operations related to product volumes and qualities. On the other hand, GENERAL management tend to be concerned with future planning and future operations, and more general policies which in themselves do not add value to specific products on a day to day basis: consequently items such as general management salaries are usually kept away from product costs, and are charged to the Profit and Loss Account in the period in which they are incurred, rather than in the period in which production units happen to be sold. Product cost is transferred in the nominal (or general) ledger from Finished Goods Stock Account to Cost of Sales Account and thence to Profit and Loss Account at the time when the goods are sold. Period costs such as general management salaries will be credited to reduce the Bank Account and charged (debited) to Cost of Sales Account and thence to the Profit and Loss Account in the period when incurred.

There are, then, a considerable number of costs which, although not classified as a direct labour or direct material, should certainly be regarded as product costs because they are incurred in bringing stock to its 'present condition and location'. The general term used for such costs is 'overheads'. Overheads are accumulated at the various cost centres in which production activity takes place. Some of this overhead can be collected there quite easily, (foremen's salaries, depreciation of machines belonging to only one cost centre) while other costs which are equally a part of product costs are charged to these cost centres by re-apportionment means (works canteen for example, the costs of which might be re-apportioned to 'customer' cost centres in proportion to their respective employee head-counts (numbers)). When *all* appropriate overheads have been collected at the points where the products are to be found, the overheads are divided by the products to derive an overhead rate.

Selecting a Fair Rate According to Circumstances

To ensure justice in the way that overheads are spread to products, the latter are described in terms of some measure of activity which is considered overhead cost provoking. For example, in a manual department, production activity might be expressed as a quantity of direct labour hours. The production of 20 handmade chairs would be described as a number of direct labour hours' worth of production and the chairs would be valued at a total cost of (a) any direct materials coded via stores requisitions to those chairs, (b) any direct labour wages costs coded through time sheets or wages analysis to those chairs, (c) (total expected departmental overhead costs ÷ total expected direct labour hours to be worked on all departmental activity) × number of direct labour hours to make those chairs.

Again, the 20 chairs might be produced in a machine-based department where many overheads were related to machine costs such as power, maintenance and depreciation. In such a case, the 20 chairs would be described as a number of machine hours' worth of production and would be charged with (a) and (b) above plus: (c) (total expected departmental overhead costs ÷ total expected machine hours to be worked on all departmental activity) × number of machine hours to make those chairs. The chairs could alternatively be 'converted' to a number of direct labour pounds (£s) worth of production, with the total production denominator being expressed as a total cost of departmental direct labour. Again, 'prime cost' is sometimes used as the basis for attracting overheads, or direct material pounds (£s). Where money values are used, a rise in pay scales or material cost rates can attract more overheads to a particular job or product, although actual overhead costs may not have risen. Industry generally appreciates that the passing of *time* is a cause of many overhead costs, and so the attaching of overheads to particular products or jobs on the basis of how much *time* they have taken tends to be looked upon as providing a truer reflection of cost.

An ideal way of confirming your understanding of methods of overhead application to saleable activity is to envisage a particular industry and simulate the charging of overheads to the activity concerned: by way of illustration we could use the construction industry. Direct material would be charged through use of prime documents such as stores requisitions and purchase invoices to particular contracts. Consequently, the overheads of the construction company could be recovered against contracts *by charging each with an overhead rate for every direct material £ charged*. The total activity for a period would be anticipated in advance as a number of pounds' worth of direct material and this would be divided into the overhead cost total expected to arise during that period. Each time someone charged one pound to a contract for direct materials, a further charge would be made for overheads using the result of the above division sum.

Such a rate could have the advantage that material control, transportation, handling and processing could be the cause of a high proportion of overheads so that it might be firmly rooted in justice and common sense: the higher the material value, the greater the proportion of the company's total overheads charged. It would be likely that strict accounting control would be maintained over materials directly charged to each construction contract through coding of material requisitions, purchase invoices and goods received notes. At the same time materials used would be capable of measurement through surveyors' reports, etc and stock control systems would be in operation. Consequently the overhead recovery system would have a sound base of documentation, recording and control as its foundation. As direct material costs would probably be already calculated and prominently reported at regular intervals, an overhead rate per £ of direct materials would have the advantages of simplicity, ease and speed of reporting.

Some Problems

Disadvantages, however, weigh heavily on the argument. In multi-contract situations some contracts could involve expensive materials which were light-weight and/or easy to handle or process. The costs of expensive projects would therefore be liable to further compounding, to the advantage of those using cheaper materials. Complications could arise as to whether direct materials charged and on site were appropriate as the basis for overhead recovery, or direct materials actually absorbed through processing into project work-in-progress. This would be particularly relevant when many overheads were incurred in delivering materials to sites and in protecting and securing unworked materials.

The timing of overhead charges to particular contracts could be influenced by deliveries of material which often take place at a very early stage, and well before overheads were actually incurred. Consequently the amount of (1) the credit balance on a construction company's Overhead Applied Account (with a debit to Work-in-Progress Account), and (2) the debit to the Overhead Control Account (with a credit to such accounts as Bank Account), could be out-of-step for long periods. This might provoke time-consuming enquiries, and precipitate premature accounting adjustments: an overhead control account balance and its applied account counterpart could be set off against each other and any resulting difference spun off as a variance to a new nominal ledger account. In the environment of the construction industry, the charging of overheads based on direct material costs could result also in a fairly high level of uncertified 'work completed': overhead cost charges could be entered in contract accounts very soon after direct material charges, giving the work-in-progress account in the nominal ledger a 'finished' appearance while the evidence on site indicated that projects concerned were far from complete.

The above problems are far from insurmountable, and quite often a final decision is taken to charge contracts with an overhead recovery rate per £ of direct material charged.

A construction company may decide alternatively to use a direct labour recovery rate: then a choice has to be made between a predetermined activity level expressed as direct labour *pounds* or as direct labour *hours*. In either case, there is the advantage of the recovery system again being based on established, well-used recording and control procedures. In addition, a very high proportion of total labour costs are likely to be classified as direct, ie involving time spent directly on specific contracts in a measurable way. The need to create new accounting analysis procedures for splitting direct and indirect labour is likely to be minimal; and a rate based on direct labour activity is easily understood. Overheads applied to contracts (debits to Work-in-Progress and credits to Overhead Applied Account) and actual overheads incurred (debits to Overhead Control Account and credits to Bank Account, etc) may often be closely in line, as many overheads emanate from the presence of direct labour on site rather than the presence of materials which may or may not be under processing or in use.

In selecting a rate per £ of direct labour or a rate per direct labour hour, it should be remembered that many overheads are provoked by time spent by operatives and are not truly reflected by the amount of wages paid. For example, there might be five operatives on contract A for a total of 10 hours each, being paid on average £4 per hour, and five for the same time on contract B, being paid £3·50. If total direct wages were budgeted at £10,000, and overheads recoverable totalled £5,000, contract A would be charged $5 \times 10 \times £4 \times \frac{£5,000}{10,000} = £100$, and contract B $5 \times 10 \times £3·50 \times \frac{£5,000}{10,000} = £87·50$. This would penalise contract A which would suffer extra overheads not because of extra time spent but because of the technical difference in wage rates. In some companies the choice between direct labour pounds and direct labour hours as a measure of activity would be a vital issue in ensuring true and fair valuation of contract work in progress, while in others which had parity of wage rates and operating conditions, the decision as to which rate to use might be made in favour of whichever was the simpler method.

In any event, every company must measure its activity for accounting periods in terms of some unit (such as direct labour hours) for the purposes of spreading overhead costs over that activity, and must also total overheads costs so that the latter may be divided by the former to obtain a rate per unit of activity.

Separate Recovery Rates for Fixed and Variable Costs

Separate recovery rates are often prepared for (a) those overheads which are *variable*, ie which increase in total with increases in activity and decline in sympathy with reductions in activity levels, and (b) those which are *fixed*, ie which are incurred and chargeable simply because a department has existed as an operational unit for a period of time; the amount of fixed costs does not fluctuate in sympathy with activity levels. An example of (a) would be electrical power in a machine-based department, and of (b), the foreman's salary.

Presenting Control Reports

In such cases, two lists of overhead costs for a period are prepared; the first covering variable costs, the second, fixed costs. Variable and fixed costs are divided in turn by the chosen budgeted activity level for the period, and separate rates of application are calculated. Should actual activity differ from budget, the fixed overhead rate will be used for each actual unit produced, so over- or under-absorption of fixed costs will ensue. For example, suppose that a company expected (budgeted) to make 100 units of a product; direct materials were budgeted at £200, direct labour at £400, variable production overheads at £300. Fixed production overheads for the period were expected to be £500. Stock was to be valued at full cost (ie including fixed production costs). In practice, 120 units were made, costing £280, £430 and £400 for direct materials, direct labour and variable production overheads respectively. Actual raw material costs represented 125 units purchased and used at £2·24 each. The original budgeted cost of £200 comprised 100 units at a standard cost of £2 each. Direct labour actually involved 215 hours at £2 each, while the original budgeted cost of £400 comprised 200 hours at £2 each. Actual fixed production overheads were £480. The company expected to sell all production at £20 per unit, but in practice the 120 units made were each sold for £19. This simple case will serve to illustrate the importance of separation of fixed and variable costs for cost control purposes, to enable management to react prudently to cost deviations. The company's operating results could be presented as follows:

Company —— : Operating Statement for Period ——

Line Ref.		(1) Original Budget Units	(1) £	(2) Flexing adjustment because of activity change Units	(2) £	(3) Revised budgeted results for actual activity Units	(3) £	(4) Actual results at actual activity Units	(4) £	(5) Variances affecting profits (F = favourable U = unfavourable) (a) Sales Price	(b) Fixed cost Volume	(c) Fixed cost expenditure	(d) Variable cost	(e) Sales Volume col(2)	(f) Total
1	Sales	100	2,000	20	400	120	2,400	120	2,280	120(U)					120(U)
	Cost of Production	100		20		120		120							
2	Direct materials	200		40		240		280					40(U)		40(U)
3	Direct labour	400		80		480		430					50(F)		50(F)
4	Variable production overheads	300		60		360		400					40(U)		40(U)
5	Fixed production overheads	500		100		600		480			100(F)	20(F)			120(F)
6											(Note 1)				
											(Note 2)				
7	Total available for sale	100	1,400	20	280	120	1,680	120	1,590						
8	Less: closing stock	—		—		—		—							
9	Cost of sales	100	1,400	20	280	120	1,680	120	1,590					120(F)	120(F)
10	Profit	100	600	20	120	120	720	120	690						
11	Profit Variance									120(U)	100(F)	20(F)	30(U)	120(F)	90(F)

Note 1   This amount is analysed in the ensuing summary of journal entries, into rate and usage elements.

Note 2   This amount is attributed to a variation between actual and planned efficiency in the ensuing summary of journal entries.

Company —— : Comments on Operating Statement for Period —

The linch-pin of cost control for variable costs is direct comparison at lines 3, 4 and 5 between columns (3) and (4). Budgeted and actual costs are being compared at the same *actual* activity level of 120 units. To raise alarms through comparing, say, actual direct material costs of £280 against budgeted costs of £200 (column (1)) would be thoroughly misleading, as the comparison would be distorted by the changed activity level. The extent of the *real* variable cost problems are shown at column 5(d), where in net effect, the company has spent £30 more on variable costs than the stock produced is worth in terms of its variable cost content.

When a system of standard costing is in operation, actual quantities held in stock are evaluated at standard costs, for nominal ledger, trial balance and balance sheet purposes. Differences between standard cost and actual costs incurred are shown on variance accounts in the nominal ledger, according to cause; balances on variance accounts are transferred to the profit and loss (ledger) account at the close of the accounting period concerned.

Cost control for fixed costs is shown at line 6. A rate of £5 per unit of production has been predetermined at column (1). $\left[\dfrac{£500}{100 \text{ units}}\right]$. This rate has been used the requisite number of times according to actual production quantities [120 units]. Therefore, instead of producing £500 worth of stock in terms of fixed cost content, the company has achieved £600 worth of stock (column (3)). The budget for fixed costs has been over-absorbed by £100. Supposing that the actual fixed costs, (column (4)), had been as planned: £500. The company would have had a balance sheet situation whereby stock would have increased over the period by £600 while cash would have been depleted by £500. The situation prior to sales being achieved would have been as follows:

	Extract from Budgeted Balance Sheet £	Extract from Actual Balance Sheet £
Sources of Funds		
Profit and Loss Account.	NIL	100
Uses of Funds		
Stock on hand at standard	500	600
(fixed cost element only)		
Bank/(minus)	(500)	(500)
	NIL	100

The company have the ability to go to market with 120 units worth £600 (fixed cost element) for a cash decline of £500. They can recognise this satisfactory state of affairs at time of production: there is no need to wait until the point of sale. For the purposes of this illustration we have to assume that the valuation of £600 is recoverable from customers and that the auditors are agreeable to standard costs being applied in the balance sheet. Very often, examiners confirm these assumptions by making the categorical statement: 'Value stock at full standard cost'.

Now, in reality, the actual fixed costs were £480 (column (4)). The true balance sheet situation shows:

	Extract from Budgeted Balance Sheet £	Extract from Actual Balance Sheet £
Sources of Funds		
Profit and Loss Account.	NIL	120
Uses of Funds		
Stock on hand at standard	500	600
(fixed cost element only)		
Bank/(minus)	(500)	(480)
	NIL	120

Simply by setting the wheels in motion to recover a budgeted cost of £500, using a rate of £5 per unit, the company absorbed £20 more than was necessary to convert cash minus into stock plus. So had the actual cost of £480 been accurately pre-determined, and the actual output of 120 units, a unit rate of $\frac{£480}{120} = £4$ would have been used: the result would have been:

	Extract from Budgeted Balance Sheet £	Extract from Actual Balance Sheet £
Sources of Funds		
Profit and Loss Account.	NIL	NIL
Uses of Funds		
Stock on hand at standard	480	480
(fixed cost element only)		
Bank/(minus)	(480)	(480)
	NIL	NIL

After all, the company should not be taking profit before it is earned! The raison d'être of the above approach must be (I repeat) that the examiners are insisting that stock should be valued at standard cost. What the company in consequence is doing is anticipating that it has an asset capable of recovering £600 from customers for an outlay of £480. In due course, at time of sale, a *further* £120 (column (2) total) will be gained, as a result of *selling* 20 more units than budgeted. Notice that £100 has been included in column (2) at line 7, to uplift cost of sales to £280. This measure prevents compounding or duplication of the £100 gain at line 6, column 5(b), again at column (2) line 10.

Fixed Costs are not Flexed

Hopefully, then, you will agree that I am not flexing fixed costs at line 6, column (2), but rather stock valuation, because the company had more stock on the shelves than planned. I could hardly point to 120 units of production and claim that it was worth the same as 100 units. Moreover, *because* fixed costs must *not* be flexed, but remain static at changing activity levels, I am able to

19

claim a gain (favourable variance) of £100 at column 5(b). I can anticipate holding stock worth £600 for an outlay of £500. The fact that actual fixed costs were £480 affords a *further* gain of £20 at 5(c).

Nominal (General) Ledger Entries

It would do no harm to show typical accounting steps taken throughout the nominal (or general) ledger in reaching the above results.

(1) *Direct materials*
Information on direct material purchases is normally captured (*a*) from invoices and (*b*) from stores requisitions and entered in the books of account along the following lines:

(a) Raw Material Stock at standard	Debit £250	
125 units @ £2 each		
Raw Material Price Variance	Debit £30	
125 units @ 24p		
(Say) Bank Account	Credit	£280
125 units @ £2·24		
(b) Work-in-Progress	Debit £240	
120 units @ £2		
Raw Material Usage Variance A/c	Debit £10	
5 units @ £2		
Raw Material Stock at Standard	Credit	£250

(2) *Direct Labour*
The initial reaction to actual costs is to post them to a wages 'suspense' or control account (see (a) below): entry (b) emanates from analysis of time sheets.

(a) Wages Control Account	Debit £430	
Bank Account	Credit	£430
(b) Work-in-Progress Account	Debit £480	
Standard entitlement		
$\frac{120}{100} \times 200$ hours $\times$ £2		
Direct Labour Efficiency Variance	Credit	£50
(240–215) hours $\times$ £2		
Wages Control Account	Credit	£430

(3) *Variable Production Overheads*
Expenditure classified as variable overheads originates in the books of accounts when cash book, purchase day book, petty cash book, expense claim documentation and wages sheets are analysed and coded.

(a) Variable Overhead Control Account	Debit £400	
(Say) Bank Account	Credit	£400
(b) Work-in-Progress Account at standard	Debit £360	
Variable Overhead Applied	Credit	£360
(c) Variable Overhead Applied	Debit £360	
Variable Overhead Cost Variance	Debit £40	
Variable Overhead Control	Credit	£400

You will see from the above journal entries that the Control and Applied Accounts are finally set against each other at (c). Precise, pre-determined standards would have resulted in a nil variance, meaning that a cash decline of £400 had been exactly converted to a stock increase of £400.

(4) *Fixed Production Overheads*
The same analyses as described at (3) above result in certain expenditure being classed as fixed production overhead.

(a)	Fixed Production Overhead Control	Debit £480	
	(Say) Bank Account	Credit	£480

(b) Work-in-Progress A/c at standard
120 units $\times \dfrac{£500}{100}$ Debit £600

Fixed Overhead Applied   Credit   £600

(c)	Fixed Overhead Applied	Debit £600	
	Fixed Overhead Control	Credit	£480
	Fixed Overhead Total Variance	Credit	£120

(d) Fixed Overhead Total Variance   Debit £120
Fixed Overhead Volume Variance   Credit   £100
(120–100) × £5 per unit
Fixed Overhead Expenditure Variance   Credit   £20
£(500–480)

At this stage, a trial balance would appear as follows:

	Debit	Credit	Operating Statement
	£	£	Reference
Bank Account (overdraft)		1,590	
Work-in-Progress (at standard)	1,680		Line 7, col (3)
Direct Material Price Variance	30 ⎫		Line 3, col 5(d)
Direct Material Usage Variance	10 ⎭		
Direct Labour Efficiency Variance		50	Line 4, col 5(d)
Variable Overhead Cost Variance	40		Line 5, col 5(d)
Fixed Overhead Volume Variance		100	Line 6, col 5(b)
Fixed Overhead Expenditure Variance		20	Line 6, col 5(c)
	£1,760	£1,760	

As soon as the green light is given that production is complete, the following journal entry would be authorised, to ensure that the books of account were maintained on a par with the physical facts:

Finished Goods Control Account	Debit £1,680	
Work-in-Progress Account	Credit	£1,680

The achievement of sales would result in another transfer:

Cost of Sales Account (at standard)	Debit £1,680	
Finished Goods Control Account	Credit	£1,680

Then:

Debtors Control Account	Debit £2,280	
Sales Price Variance 120 × £(20–19)	Debit £120	
Sales at Standard	Credit	£2,400

The trial balance situation would then be:

	Debit £	Credit £
Bank Account (overdraft)		1,590
Cost of Sales at Standard	1,680	
Sales at Standard		2,400
Debtors	2,280	
Sales Price Variance	120	
Direct Material Price Variance	30 }	
Direct Material Usage Variance	10	
Direct Labour Efficiency Variance		50
Variable Overhead Cost Variance	40	
Fixed Overhead Volume Variance		100
Fixed Overhead Expenditure Variance		20
	£4,160	£4,160

Any nominal ledger account balances relating to trading operations would then be transferred to the Profit and Loss Account by journal entry:

(a) Profit and Loss Account   Debit £1,880
    £(1680 + 120 + 30 + 10 + 40)

Cost of Sales at Standard	Credit	£1,680
Sales Price Variance	Credit	£ 120
Direct Material Price Variance	Credit	£ 30
Direct Material Usage Variance	Credit	£ 10
Variable Overhead Cost Variance	Credit	£ 40

(b)

Sales at Standard	Debit £2,400	
Direct Labour Efficiency Variance	Debit £ 50	
Fixed Overhead Volume Variance	Debit £ 100	
Fixed Overhead Expenditure Variance	Debit £ 20	
Profit and Loss Account	Credit	£2,570

    £(2400 + 50 + 100 + 20)

The closing trial balance would appear as follows:

	Debit £	Credit £	Operating Statement Reference
Profit and Loss Account		690	Line 10, col (4)
Bank Account (overdraft)		1,590	
Debtors	2,280		Line 1, col (4)
	2,280	2,280	

22

Cost control therefore involves marshalling costs along the trading cycle, from the earliest stages in which basic documentation is first entered in ledger accounts, to the closing episodes involving sales and cost of sales accounts. Fundamental to success is the recognition of actual activity levels so that ledger entries reflect actual physical situations, and balances on ledger accounts are compatible with tangible, visible 'shop-floor' evidence.

The Selection of Additional Activities

Management accountants should identify the costs not only of products or jobs, but also of exercising possible business options such as (a) the widening of a product range, (b) taking in sub-contracting work, (c) repairing or manufacturing tooling for third parties or (d) providing computer time or services such as management consultancy. They should identify additional saleable activity which will generate new income at little or no extra cost. For example, a particular department which suffered from under-utilisation of capacity might be able to absorb additional work at very little extra cost, with its 'fixed' labour force being paid regardless of precise capacity levels used, and with raw materials either being utilised or written off at scrap value. Another department might be able to accept new work only if (a) additional labour costs were incurred either through recruitment or through internal transfer which damaged the company's capabilities in other fields, (b) additional raw materials were purchased, the costs of which would have been otherwise avoided, (c) new plant, tooling or equipment were purchased.

In controlling costs, therefore, distinctions between fixed and variable costs, and simple analysis by cost centre and by product are insufficient. The management accountant must identify business options for future actions and prepare cost evaluations of each. In this respect the separation of costs which, at the time of assessment, are 'committed' or 'unavoidable' from those which will only damage bank balances if *particular* options are chosen is of the essence.

2 Accounting Codes

An accounting code is a series of alphabetical and/or numerical symbols, each of which represents a descriptive title in a cost, income, asset, liability or statistical classification.

When an accounts code list is introduced, (perhaps covering among other things a company's nominal ledger accounts, so that each might have, say, a five-digit numeric code), re-design of books and prime documents such as purchase orders may be necessary, especially when the number of digits forming codes is amplified or reduced from the number previously in use, or if narrative titles were previously used to the exclusion of codes.

Accounting Codes Manual

There is also a need for staff training and careful definition of terminology; usually an accounting codes manual will be issued to clarify areas of doubt. Each code will be given a full descriptive title, and the parameters of each code's scope will be defined. For example, a list of expense classification codes might be in use, for the purposes of analysing cost centre performance reports, with items such as salaries, employee travelling expenses, training costs, etc each being given a separate expense classification code. Care would be needed to clarify whether 'salaries' included or excluded payroll overhead costs such as company superannuation contributions. Again, there might be confusion as to whether temporary typing wages should be included under 'Salaries' or as part of another typical expense classification, 'Office Services'; the manual would clear any such possible anomalies.

There should be a sensible approach to timing as regards innovation dates. For example, while 1st January might seem an obvious choice of date for the introduction of a new code structure, especially if it coincided with the start of a new accounting year, accounting staff would probably be heavily committed to completion of the preceding year's accounts, and unable to give proper attention to the new codes at that time.

The balances of the preceding accounting period, in the old code format, would require re-structuring to the new. Normally a company must arrange a period of parallel running between old and new codes, whereby each transaction is coded in both the old and new formats for several accounting periods, and sets of accounts and other reports are prepared from each; this arrangement must continue until the company is satisfied that the props can be taken from under the new codes, and that they can stand alone as the basis for future accounting.

Structured Codes

The possibility of structuring codes, so that each digit has a particular significance should be considered especially by larger organisations. For example, the first digit of a sales ledger account code could be used to denote the country of the customer concerned. Again, when building a finished product code structure, a six-digit code framework might be chosen, in which, in respect of each finished product, the first digit could indicate product group, the second and third product number within product group, the fourth product quality, the fifth the manufacturing source location, and the sixth the customer category or group.

Code structuring facilitates group or company-wide summarisation and analysis. Before structuring is accepted, full analysis of what information is needed normally takes place on a very comprehensive basis. A degree of flexibility can be introduced in that one or two digits may be non-standardised or free for local use by particular managers to suit local circumstances. However, operating conditions can change significantly, and unless changes are forecast accurately and well in advance, structured frameworks can collapse. For example, the number of debtors in a company's debtors' ledger could double in the event of a merger: in such cases there is the danger of insufficient digits being available for the increased number of customer accounts.

Again, as time passes, there are generally more and more claims at local operating levels for 'special case' treatment, ie for local use of certain digits for parochial purposes. Finally, the desire to satisfy a wide range of reporting needs often results in a multi-digit, complicated code framework.

The use of blocks of codes with each block serving further analysis needs can be considered an alternative to structuring. For example, if a company had 4,000 customers across various countries, a fifth digit could be provided for country numbers. An alternative would be to retain a four digit code for customers, but provide blocks: 1–2,000 UK; 2,001–2,200 France, etc.

Areas Covered by Accounting Codes

The types of accounting codes which would be considered for inclusion in an accounts code manual would cover: (1) the nominal ledger; (2) expense classifications or elements of cost; (3) raw material stocks; (4) production and service department cost centres; (5) finished goods stocks; (6) currencies; (7) countries; (8) companies (within a group); (9) locations (within a group or a company); (10) sales areas; (11) customers; (12) creditors; (13) product groups; (14) customer categories or ultimate user categories, (when for example, it was necessary to know the type of industry to which particular products were destined).

Numeric Digits

When computer-based or other mechanised accounting systems are in use, numeric digits are ideal for saving time. Data input in this format can be quickly punched onto cards or magnetic tape, etc and the computer or other data processing equipment involved can read, convert, store, retrieve, process and produce it thereafter at incredible speed.

The Use of Edit Routines within Computer-based Reporting Systems

The accounting codes used within batches of input data to management information systems can be 'edited' (or checked) by computer to identify potential errors. Thus a business transaction coded to a particular cost centre and to the expense class 'travel expenses' might be rejected by a computer unless the input data for the transaction also showed an employee code. Similarly, a charge made to a raw material stores control account in a nominal ledger might be queried through use of an edit routine unless input included a raw material stock account number essential for maintaining stockholding records in a computer-based subsidiary ledger.

3   Budgets and Budgetary Control

The Institute of Cost and Management Accountants has defined a budget as: 'A financial and/or quantitative statement, prepared and approved prior to a defined period of time, of the policy to be pursued during that period for the purpose of attaining a given objective. It may include income, expenditure and the employment of capital.' The preparation of budgets forces management to take a long, lingering look at what the future holds. Budgets are prepared for each business or commercial function (such as production, selling and distribution), and are the responsibility of specific managers. This means that they involve 'crystal ball gazing' on future levels of activity as well as levels of expense. Activity and expense levels tend to be inter-linked, in that if activity changes, some costs, the variable ones, will move up or down in sympathy.

Selecting a Unit of Measure

Those who are responsible for the preparation of budgets firstly require some unit of measure for activity which is planned, which will provide a meaningful indication of the effort to be expended by the resources available. This measure may be a number of products varnished, invoices processed, orders activated, computer hours run, hours open for business, meals served, direct labour hours worked, and so on. When the unit of measure has been selected, each of the elements of cost within the jurisdiction of the manager preparing a budget should be tested for its reaction to changes in activity levels. (It is seldom possible, by the way, to structure the elements of cost in such a way that each is entirely variable or entirely fixed. Telephone costs in a sales office provide an example, the rentals being fixed and the calls variable. Repairs and maintenance costs in a factory involve partly preventive maintenance and servicing (fixed) and other repair expense which changes in sympathy with activity levels (variable).)

Expense is Related to an Activity Level

The primary task is identification of *production* activity through the use of measures which may vary from manufacturing department to department, eg 'tonnes' in department A, 'lengths' in B and 'metres' in C. To make production budgets possible substantial support is required from 'service' departments which do not in themselves directly add saleable value to end products. Each of these departments, such as stores, internal transport, works personnel, works accounting etc. should, at budget preparation time, agree a level of physical support for the production function and should have this authorised. Thus, a stores department might agree to have 100,000 cubic feet available, maintained and serviced for raw material supplies. A maintenance department might arrange to have 5,000 maintenance man-hours available. These levels of clearly identified physical measures would then require authentication by being absorbed into budgets attested by senior management. Thereafter, monetary evaluations of these levels of service would be agreed. The *need* for and level of the service would come first, and the monetary implications second.

Alternative Measures of Activity

It is important to realise that the budget of a production department or cost centre may be expressed as a 'number of chairs' for a period, but in order to attach overheads equitably to particular chairs, they *may* be converted to a number of hours' equivalent, and overhead cost attached at a rate per hour. Records have then to be kept on the number of hours taken for each chair. Many companies would, however, define the activity level as a number of hours from start to finish during budgetary procedures.

Flexing Budgets

Without the separation of fixed and variable expense, there is a very real danger of trying to make sense of a straight comparison, in due course, of budgeted (allowed) expense at one level of activity with the actual expense at another. A reliable assessment of which expenses are in fact variable enables management to 'flex' the comparison and thus control expense levels by taking action on any variances between actual and budgeted expense for actual activity levels.

The actual cost incurred by a manager can be measured against his cost entitlement if variable and fixed costs have been separated. It is very important to choose a measure of activity increases or decreases in the level of which cause a high proportion of costs to vary. If we were to take a sales office as an example, such a cost centre might decide to use pounds of sales (sterling) as a unit of measure. If the budgeted level of activity were agreed as £100,000 of sales the budgeted expense might be assessed as, say, 4p per £1 of sales plus £20,000 fixed expense for the period. This would mean that the manager would be entitled to spend a budget of £20,000 for the budget period regardless of actual sales achieved, to cover such items as office rates, cleaning, heating and lighting and the salaries of office staff who were an integral part of any activity at all, *plus* 4p for each £1 of sales achieved.

Now if actual sales in the budget period were £150,000, the manager could claim an entitlement or budget of 150,000 × 4p of variable overheads, and could not be criticised if his variable expense total reached £6,000. The sales increase, however, could easily have been caused by an increase in selling prices. Such a cause would not bring in its wake any actual variable overhead cost increase. The same amount of effort would go into processing the same number of orders, invoices, letters, telephone calls, etc. Thus the manager would receive a 'buffer' or 'cushion' of cost entitlement of £(150,000–100,000) × 4p = £2,000. A more sensitive measure of activity would have been 'number of sales orders processed'. This would have involved re-appraising each element of cost in the light of this new measure, and attributing expense which varied with orders processed, as a new rate of pence per order processed. Expenses which failed this new sensitivity test would be fixed and would again be allocated to the cost centre as a set amount for the period.

The actual activities of manufacturing service departments such as stores or maintenance may well vary from planned levels, and the management accountant should separate costs of having a servicing facility at all from those which will rise and fall in sympathy with activity levels. In this way, sensible attitudes may be formulated when, say, storekeepers' wages rise dramatically because 'the factory is busy', and maintenance department costs are unchanged when production capacity utilisation has dropped from, say, 80% to 70%. Again, a string of questions such as 'If the company shed 20% of its workforce, what costs other than wages could be saved?' might need to be addressed. Any departments which had previously settled on 'man-hours' as their measure of activity might well find such a question comparatively easy to answer.

Reasons for Variations in Unit Costs

It is an over-simplification to assert that variable costs per unit of activity stay at a constant per unit rate for all levels of activity, eg that if it is expected that the first chair will cost, say, £8 for variable costs, the nineteenth should therefore cost £8. There are many factors which cause costs to vary, quite apart from changes in activity levels: there may, for example, be changes in operating conditions after a certain level of activity has been reached. The incidence of scrap, or of machine breakdown may rise disproportionately beyond a certain activity level. Poorly trained operatives may be 'roped in' after a certain level, causing the same costs to be spread over fewer output units.

Comprehensive Budget Preparation

The preparation of budgets is achieved as a joint effort by the management of all the functions of a business. Determining one particular budget in isolation would be similar to the preparation by a private individual of, say, a 'clothing budget' or a 'holiday budget'. One thing leads logically to another; the individual would quickly find that clothing or holiday plans depended on an income budget, and on the demands on that income by other expenditure items. Before long a cash flow budget would be involved, to avoid embarrassing peaks and troughs in cash availability. So in business a set of budgets is prepared to enable management to harmonise their efforts and to ensure that all the other business functions mobilise their resources to keep up the pace set by what is known as the 'leader' budget.

The Role of the 'Leader' Budget

The leader budget is the spearhead of any progress which an organisation is intending to make during the budget period. Management usually meet to select the leader budget and to ensure its contents are challenging and that they set a fast but attainable pace for the others to follow. Whoever is responsible for sales (of goods or services) is of course a contender for this important position. In many cases the market for what the organisation has to offer is the limiting factor, ie production capacity exceeds market demand, and the capacity to distribute the end product outweights the size of the distribution task. In such instances the sales function becomes the leader because it would be wasteful for production to provide more than could be sold. Problems arise when market demand is greater than the ability to produce, and decisions have to be taken as to whether production sets the pace, albeit a slower one than the usurped sales would have liked. If the leader function sets a slow pace, the other functions need to slip-stream behind and must not overtake. This can mean under-utilisation of resources. For example, if expensive new machines are installed, but the market demand is eroded for one reason or another, a Sales Director might stipulate only a tiny percentage increase in an ensuing budget period, or no increase at all. Consequently production would need to limit capacity usage, but force a limited output of finished goods to bear the cost of depreciating, servicing and having available much more equipment than had been properly employed. In these circumstances the Sales Director would naturally be under severe pressure to step up his marketing plans.

Flexibility in budgetary control is essential, however, as forecasting is so difficult, and as it would be nonsense to compare the budgeted use of resources at the budgeted level of activity with the actual use at another (actual) level.

Sequence of Preparation

There is a preparation sequence for budgets, one function following another until a budgeted (or projected) balance sheet is finally possible which will show the organisation's state of affairs at the close of the budget period.

The list below appears in the correct preparation sequence. It is assumed that there is enough production capacity to provide for sales demand:
 (1) Sales budget (quantities and values)
 (2) Production budget (quantities)
 (3) Direct material purchases budget
 (4) Direct labour budget
 (5) Factory overhead budgets (can be split between variable and fixed)
 (6) Cost of production budget
 (7) Cost of goods sold budget
 (8) Closing stock budget
 (9) Selling and administration budgets
 (10) Budgeted statement of cash receipts and payments
 (11) Budgeted operating statement/trading account
 (12) Budgeted balance sheet.

Background Factors in Budget Preparation

A sensible sales budget depends upon a detailed knowledge of production capacity available to convert customers' orders into real saleable goods or services. In other words, there is no point in anticipating a particular level of sales achievement unless there is a production capability to make it possible. Misjudgement of production capacity is a frequent cause of over-runs on cost (eg through having to work overtime to achieve customer deadlines) and of failure to secure repeat orders (through letting customers down on delivery dates).

Another pitfall lies in failure to measure the distinction between ideal (or maximum) capacity and (net) practical capacity. Thus the professional joiner who thinks of his 'working day' as from 8.00 a.m. until 5.00 p.m. will incur the wrath of customers when he fails to deduct from it a reasonable proportion to allow for severe traffic jams en route from home to customers' premises. His 'budgeted sales' or anticipated earnings will be inflated to include work which he will not have enough time to handle.

Perhaps the greatest danger in budgeting lies in failure to measure the work content in particular jobs, products or processes. Such shortcomings result in having insufficient or excessive resources available in support, frequently of the wrong types and at inappropriate times. Many organisations indulge in monetary evaluations before associated physical events have been defined and organised.

Requests for financial support by way of short or middle term loans are often based on budget projections of the future. A range of factors should be taken into consideration when each of the above budgets is prepared, so that in due course the validity of the plans upon which loan security may depend can be tested. In particular, because the sales budget is normally a corner-stone, a brief list of factors which would be important is shown below:

(a) Previous year's performance
(b) Competitor action
(c) Market research
(d) Reports by sales force
(e) Recent customer reactions
(f) Outstanding order book
(g) Pricing policies and agreed price levels
(h) Sales training progress and future plans
(i) Government legislation
(j) Product image
(k) Long-term trends
(l) Customer plans/customer credit-worthiness.

The Need to Set a Fast Pace

A budget committee is often set up representing all the functions of a business, to mould individual management aspirations into a common, total plan. The leader budget is usually chosen by this committee which also set the pace to be maintained over the budget period. Each manager initially sets targets for his own function which are unconstrained by weakness elsewhere in the organisation. For example, the sales director would not initially restrict his target sales by assuming failure by the distribution manager in finding additional trucks. The production director would not limit his activity budget on the basis that the buyer would fail to find additional materials. Everything would be put into top gear at first and excuses would be discussed in turn as to why particular targets might be impossible. Initial budgets would be set which demanded success by the other functions contributing to the overall effort.

Budget Officers

A 'budget officer' normally acts in a secretarial capacity to the budget committee. In groups of companies he will usually work as an employee of the parent (or holding) company. In any event, he will generally be located at the company's head office. Various job titles are in use, Group Budget Accountant, Management Accountant – UK Group, Group Financial Accountant being examples. He will usually report within a group directly to the Finance Director of the group's executive board, or to the Group Chief Accountant. Where no group of companies exists, the budget officer will report to the company's Finance Director or to the Chief Accountant, but, depending on company size, it might be necessary for the head of the accounting function to fill the role in person.

The budget officer's role is principally to interpret the guiding decisions of the budget committee, and to advise each executive responsible for the budget of specific activities, with a view to securing a budget which is compatible with that of other sections. This preliminary work must be done early enough to enable the final budget for the company to be agreed by the required date.

The budget officer will report directly to the budget committee, ensuring that minutes of each meeting of the committee are taken and distributed, and that the decisions therein are activated. His capacity is generally administrative, ensuring good communications, the issue of clear instructions by the committee, and adherence to timetables. The practical work of budget preparation is carried out by the executives in charge of the functions and sections involved, and their link with the budget committee becomes effectively the budget officer.

Steps to Facilitate Budget Preparation

The preparation of budgets is of course a lengthy task and the image of budgets may often become tarnished with the passing of time. Various measures can be taken to ensure that budget preparation proceeds as effectively as possible, and to eliminate a negative attitude held by staff. The undernoted checklist is written in the form of instructional 'prompts':

(1) Obtain a copy of the budget preparation timetable and check for feasibility. Compare with that of previous year to determine whether there has been any advance of deadline dates.

(2) List possible sources of grievance or complaint, eg the pressing nature of other work, lack of clarity in definition of expense classifications (or elements of cost), poor clerical coding competence, etc.

(3) List known ways in which current budgetary control system has been failing to provide necessary information for decision making. Include poor timing of reports, errors outside the agreed accuracy tolerances, and poor presentation, eg failure to highlight major variances.

(4) Where possible remove work-load bottlenecks by adjusting priorities of work interfering with the work of budget preparation. This would need to be done in full consultation with senior management for whom information reports were being prepared. This would ease immediate pressures and give at least some of the staff and management the opportunity to rediscover the advantages, latent and otherwise, of budgetary control.

(5) Explore the budgetary control framework, ie the organisation of cost (collection) centres under functional heads, and the allocation of responsibilities to specific individuals for the direct control of costs. This would earmark anomalies or uncertainties about cost centre boundaries.

(6) Ensure that the budget for each cost centre is being prepared as a constituent part of a total functional budget, which in turn is in accord with an overall master budget. The latter would be in harmony with the company's longer-term strategic objectives.

(7) (a) Determine the degree to which costs are re-apportioned one cost centre to another, and ensure that clear distinction is made in reporting formats between costs directly charged to a cost centre and those re-apportioned from other cost centres on an arbitrary, estimated basis.

(b) Confirm that the bases of re-apportionment are understood by management and that they are equitable (whether or not (a) applies).

(8) Determine whether managers are asked to explain variances between actual and budgeted expense for elements of cost over which they have no direct control.

(9) Similarly, check on the degree to which pre-determined standards are used for the apportionment of costs of service departments to manufacturing and other service department cost centres. Charges ought to be on the basis of standard or budgeted times allowed for services rendered, eg for routine repairs and maintenance. In this way, the operating cost centre receiving a charge would rightly be responsible for the overall quantity of service consumed but not directly for fluctuations in unit prices or service department efficiency; the 'customer department' would be charged at the standard worth of the job × standard rate, justifiably leaving the service department to explain its own cost variances.

(10) Check on whether charges to a specific cost centre wrongly depend on how much of the service is being consumed by other departments. This can happen if fixed costs are re-apportioned on the basis of actual usage. Very pronounced anomalies often result; for example, the fixed costs of a repair shop for a full accounting period could fall on a single 'customer' cost centre using the services offered for only 50% of the period. The following period, two customer cost centres each using repair shop for half of the total period would each receive a 50% charge. The first customer would thus receive the same service for half the fixed cost charge.

Reasons for Poor Growth

Any manager whose budget effectively slows down the projected progress intended for an organisation as a whole must of course justify any impediments. For example, suppose that a sales director says in effect that he can budget for only a 2% increase in quantities sold in an ensuing year. He would need to offer reasons. Some possible reasons appear below:

(1) Poor company image
(2) Shortage of skilled salesmen
(3) Fierce competition
(4) Recent loss of key customer
(5) Products not well known

In general excuses of the above kind, which could be offered by any of the managers present, are tested and remedial action proposed which will remove impediments to progress whenever possible.

Budgeting in Inflation

An inflationary environment offers new opportunities and threats which can be rolled together under a title of 'challenges'. Firstly, each manager must *communicate* quickly with colleagues preparing other budgets, when a significant level of inflation is impending, so that counter-measures may be taken in good time to alleviate any damage. Steps which should be considered after 'early-warning' include the exploitation of alternative (substitute) raw materials and/or sources of supply, the abandonment of certain finished products which might be subject to customer resistance, and new-marketing methods to try to break down such resistance. Secondly, cost analysis and control take on new significance. For example, each element of cost such as rates, insurance and salaries is likely to have its own inflation rate. If a company has a sound understanding of the cost specifications of its products or services, the effects of inflation on forthcoming costs can be monitored.

In general terms, the words 'substitute product' are perhaps the most significant which can be used in budgeting for inflation. For example, many restaurants have now introduced 'carry-out' services to combat inflation, and even hotels at the top-end of the market have built self-catering chalets in their grounds.

Finally, inflation requires an assessment of each business transaction against *three* yardsticks, namely: (1) profitability, (2) liquidity and (3) productivity. For example, a sale included in a budget might enhance profitability yet be achieved (a) only through offering excessive credit, thus making it poor on liquidity, (b) because the customer is at a disadvantage through not having competitors' quotes: sales achieved despite poor productivity are frequently short-lived.

The Role of Opportunism

A company should be prepared to consider provision of excesses of capacity above and beyond levels required to meet known requirements. These 'cushions' of capacity would, of course, attract additional expenditure, but such extra costs might be insignificant when weighed against prospects of additional sales income. For example, a company might consider purchasing a machine capable of making 120 units of production per annum despite envisaged sales of 100 units. The costs of a machine 'larger than necessary' might outweigh a smaller one as regards power, manning, supervision, maintenance, financing and depreciation. Yet these extra costs, plus, say, additional marketing expenses, might well be worthwhile if they could, somehow, lead to the achievement of sales of the extra 20 units. 'Excess capacity' although expensive, ceases to be excess if a market can be turned around with a little extra effort.

4 Product Costing and Assessing Periodic Profits

In general, profits (and losses) are appraised at the close of accounting periods. However during the day to day running of any organisation the flood-gates of expense are open. We have discussed how every expense should be directed to a cost centre for control purposes, in particular for comparison against expected expenditure. We have also learned that some kinds of expenditure can be expected to rise or fall in sympathy with activity, but that to assess this sensitivity we must know what our measure of activity is and relate each element of cost's behaviour to it.

Timing of Charges Against Profits

Students must be quite clear as to when expense, (controlled as it takes place), can be allowed to 'drop off' as a charge against a particular accounting period. 'Product' cost attaches itself to a saleable product (goods or services) and drops off as a charge against the period in which the sale of these products takes place. Thus product cost becomes 'period cost' only during the period when the sale took place. Costs which are not attached to products as product cost, attack the trading results of the period to which they relate, completely regardless of any production activity or product sales activity; they are period costs at all times. You will appreciate that the classification of a particular cost as a product cost can spell relief to a particular account period's management – if the products concerned have not been sold. In such cases the costs concerned will be charged as part of the total production costs for the period, only to be 'lifted out' as closing stock valuation! They are then 'dumped' on the doorstep of the ensuing period's management as their opening charge (opening stock valuation). If the stock of products is still unsold at the close of *this* period, it in turn will be relieved of responsibility by a further 'lift-off' of what will again by closing stock. So it will go on until a period can be found which is capable of taking the weight of this charge: capability arrives of course when sales take place which will (hopefully) more than compensate for the charge.

It must be remembered that such passing forward of product cost from period to period is only allowable insofar as it is likely to be recoverable through ultimate sales. That part of the valuation of unsold stock which is suspected of being irrecoverable travels no further than the period in which such suspicions are aroused.

Faulty or haphazard decisions about what is product cost can result in fluctuations in profits as each period's trading results are affected by ever-changing and/or erroneous reliefs or lack of reliefs. Consistency in selection of product costs is essential. It must be emphasised that product cost includes all costs which have been incurred in bringing stock to its present condition and location. Fixed costs can certainly be included, but it is essential for students to realise the possible pitfalls in relieving a particular period of its manufacturing fixed expenses on the grounds that they are product costs and relate to unsold production. Basically, when certain 'mixes' of circumstances prevail, a single period can eventually face up to two periods' fixed expenses as a charge against its profits. This could happen, for example, when period 1 had relieved itself of its fixed expenses, and period 2 had little production onto which to attach its own fixed expenses.

To meet this accounting principle regarding stock valuation, commercial and industrial organisations tend to regard manufacturing overheads as product costs, and selling, distribution and administrative overheads as period costs, but students should be able to identify possible exceptions to such a sweeping rule. The treatment of research and development cost is also worth examining.

Product Costs Under Absorption Costing

'Absorption' costing can take product costing to the advanced stage of attaching a very high proportion of total costs to individual products: every cost incurred across an organisation is

Absorption costing

spread over its end products by whichever means appear to be most equitable, provided that it can pass the test of having been incurred in bringing stock to its present condition and location. However, methods of spreading the more 'remote' costs which have been directly controlled at cost centres far removed from the scene of manufacture either in the functional or geographical sense or both, must of necessity be purely arbitrary, and a certain amount of guesswork normally applies. For example, it would be a difficult task to ensure that appropriate portions of a works director's salary were charged to each of twenty products.

Absorption costing is frequently necessary for Government contracts, where selling prices are on a total cost plus a percentage for profit. It may also be most easily applied when there are one or two similar products or perhaps a single service, eg a small taxi business.

The main danger arising from use of absorption costing is that the product costs derived may form the basis for far reaching decisions as to which products to promote and which to eliminate, management having lost sight of the fact that cost apportionments have been largely guesswork.

Proponents like to think that absorption costing acts as a sharp reminder to those whose activities and related expenditure are far removed from end products, that without products to sell which were capable of carrying such high overhead burdens, their livelihoods would not exist. This is one way of ensuring correct priorities; in particular the need to have a strong sales function becomes paramount.

Product Costs Under Marginal Costing

The alternative to absorption costing is 'marginal' or 'direct' costing, which relates to products only those costs which are directly sensitive to increases or decreases in activity levels. Marginal costing in its full-bodied sense fails to attach a full load of all those costs which are incurred in bringing stock to its present condition and location, and for this reason it exists alongside mainstream accounting systems and does not supersede them.

If marginal costing advocates carried their system as far as the annual accounts of an organisation, each accounting period would bear its own fixed expense, unsold stock valuation being at variable cost only. This would minimise any danger of off-loading uncomfortably high fixed expenses from one period (as part of closing stock) onto the ensuing period (as part of opening stock). However absorption costing advocates indicate that their costs of providing and maintaining facilities for making products are as much a part of product cost as anything else.

Cumulative Build-up of Product Costs

Products which pass through more than one manufacturing cost centre on their way to completion will collect a 'snowball' of cost. Each foreman concerned will use stores requisition slips, job cards etc to ensure that appropriate direct materials and labour are attached during a particular product's sojourn in his department. In addition, the product will be appraised in the light of the measure of activity which has been selected for each department in turn, and all overhead expenses which have been attributed to each department will be attached fairly by means of overhead recovery rates. For example, if a particular product run lasts 6 hours, it may form part of a total activity for the department estimated at 120 hours for the accounting period. If total variable overheads for the period are estimated at £1,200, the product run will have

$$6 \times \frac{1,200}{120} = £60$$ attached to it for overheads before it leaves the department.

This snowballing effect applies to individual jobs, processes, products or batches of products, but costs concerned are also summarised in 'control accounts' which form part of the nominal ledger records, and hence they feature in the trial balance and in the accounts. The pivot for all cost movement related to manufacture is the 'work-in-progress' account. Into it are charged totals of materials used (direct materials), direct wages, direct expenses, and applied variable and fixed overheads. Credits out of work in progress take place when work is completed, and transferred (debited) into 'finished goods stock' or, if there is no such intermediate stock account, into 'cost of sales'.

Nominal Ledger Entries for Each Element of Cost

The nominal or general ledger route which cost follows is normally as follows, for:

(1) direct materials:
   (a) Raw Material Store to (b) Work-in-Progress to (c) Finished Goods Store to (d) Cost of Sales.

(2) direct wages (or labour):
   (a) Wages Control to (b) Work-in-Progress to (c) Finished Goods Store to (d) Cost of Sales.

(3) overheads:
   (a) Overhead Applied to (b) Work-in-Progress to (c) Finished Goods Store to (d) Cost of Sales.

At (b) and beyond, direct materials, direct wages and overheads lose their separate identities and are absorbed as part of the balance on the account concerned.

Subsidiary Ledger Accounts for Accumulation and Control

COSTING depends on the identification of production or manufacturing departments (or cost centres), because it is there that COST OF PRODUCTION, or WORK-IN-PROGRESS is built up. This build up is totalled in the WORK-IN-PROGRESS CONTROL ACCOUNT in the nominal ledger. The use of the word CONTROL implies that a subsidiary ledger is maintained, detailing separate subsidiary ledger accounts for each job, or process or product, in the same way that a subsidiary ledger is kept for Debtors' Control Account, to detail individual sales ledger accounts.

In addition to subsidiary records for jobs, processes or products, subsidiary records should also be kept for departments or cost centres handling the work. Thus, when the Work-in-Progress Account is debited or credited in the nominal or general ledger, similar debits/credits should be made to subsidiary accounts for the product unit concerned and also the department concerned: obviously codes on prime documents such as purchase orders can become rather lengthy when they have to serve so many purposes.

Cost Categories and their Treatment

Costing categorises each cost incurred throughout an organisation as: (1) DIRECT LABOUR. (2) DIRECT MATERIALS. (3) DIRECT EXPENSES. (4) VARIABLE WORKS OVERHEAD. (5) FIXED WORKS OVERHEAD. (6) ADMINISTRATION OVERHEAD. (7) VARIABLE SELLING OVERHEAD. (8) FIXED SELLING OVERHEAD. From time to time, works overhead may not be split into variable and fixed categories. Similarly, administration and selling costs are sometimes regarded as one item. Moreover, a separate cost category may be used for DISTRIBUTION OVERHEADS – these are usually treated in the same way as (7) or (8). The following procedures are typical:

(1) *DIRECT LABOUR*
   Emanates from wages analyses: wages charged to specific jobs, processes or products are classified as direct.

Work-in-Progress Control Account	Dr
Wages Control Account	Cr

   The appropriate job, process or product should also be debited in the work-in-progress subsidiary ledger. Outside the nominal or general ledger, a further subsidiary ledger should maintain records of departments (or cost centres) handling the work in progress activity, and this should also be debited by way of a memorandum.

35

(2) *DIRECT MATERIALS*
Emanates from analyses of stores requisitions and/or the purchase day book; the latter is more appropriate if materials are earmarked for work in progress as soon as the company concerned takes possession of the goods, eg when they are off-loaded at the goods inwards department and sent straight to production.

| Work-in-Progress Control Account | Dr |
| Stores Control Account | Cr |

or

| Work-in-Progress Control Account | Dr |
| Creditors Control Account | Cr |

The same note as at the close of (1) above applies.

(3) *DIRECT EXPENSES*
Emanates from analyses of stores requisitions, purchase day book, and cash and petty cash books. Direct expenses usually constitute but a tiny fraction of total company expenditure, and indeed of work-in-progress. Perhaps the payment of professional fees when related directly to a specific end-product would serve as an illustration.

| Work-in-Progress Control Account | Dr |
| Bank (or Creditors Control) Account | Cr |

The same note as at the close of (1) applies.

(4) *VARIABLE WORKS OVERHEAD*
Emanates from analyses of stores requisitions, purchase day book, wages, cash book and petty cash book. The initial 'acid test' is whether the expense item has been incurred in 'bringing stock to its present condition and location'. Items passing the test are controlled through either a general variable works overhead control account for the factory as a whole, or through departmental variable works overhead control accounts, depending on whether variable works overhead is charged to work-in-progress (i) in stages, or (ii) at a blanket rate per unit of activity to recover all of the variable works overhead for the factory at one time.

(a) Variable Works Overhead Control
    Account   Dr
    Stores Control Account   Cr ⎫
      and/or
    Creditors Control Account   Cr ⎬ According to
      and/or   various analyses
    Wages Control Account   Cr
      and/or
    Bank Account   Cr ⎭

Then separately,

(b) Work-in-Progress Control Account   Dr
    Variable Works Overhead Control Account   Cr
      or
    Variable Works Overhead Applied Account   Cr

Re (a), there has to be a subsidiary ledger in support of the Variable Works Overhead Control Account; examples of subsidiary ledger accounts could include factory overtime premium, idle time costs and machine running costs. Re (b), the same note as at the close of (1) applies.

(5) *FIXED WORKS OVERHEAD*
Emanates from the same analyses as at (4) above. It is unlikely that the analyses of stores requisitions, however, will yield much that can be classified as fixed expense. The 'acid test' referred to at (4) should also be applied.

    (a) Fixed Works Overhead Control A/c   Dr
        Stores Control A/c   Cr
         or
        Creditors' Control A/c   Cr   According to
         or   various analyses
        Wages Control A/c   Cr
         or
        Bank A/c   Cr

Then, separately,

    (b) Work-in-Progress Control A/c   Dr
        Fixed Works Overhead Control A/c   Cr
            or
        Fixed Works Overhead Applied A/c   Cr

Again, re (a) there is a supporting subsidiary ledger. Re (b), the same note as at the close of (1) applies.

(6) *ADMINISTRATION OVERHEAD*

Depending on the nature of this category of overhead, which emanates from analyses of the purchase day book, cash book and wages, it may or may not be considered as having been incurred 'in bringing stock to its present condition and location'. For example, if much of a factory's accounting effort goes into the preparation of routine day-to-day reports on production achievement, costs and efficiency, it might be considered that the costs of running the accounting department, or a fair proportion thereof, could be included in the valuation of work-in-progress. In any event:

    (a) Administration Overhead Control A/c   Dr
        Bank A/c   Cr
         or
        Creditors' Control A/c   Cr

Then, separately,

    (b)(i) Work-in-Progress Control A/c   Dr
        Administration Overhead Control A/c   Cr
           or
        Administration Overhead Applied A/c   Cr

However, in the event of administration overhead not being regarded as incurred in bringing stock to its present condition and location, substitute (b)(ii) below for (i):

    (b)(ii) Cost of Sales A/c   Dr
        Administration Overhead Control A/c   Cr

Re (a), the rule about a subsidiary ledger applies. Re (b)(i) the same note as at the close of (1) applies.

(7) *VARIABLE SELLING OVERHEAD*

Emanates from analyses of the purchase day book, cash book, wages and petty cash book, with particular reference to employees' expenses claims analyses which are presumed to be dealt with through the cash book or petty cash book. The total of such overhead rises or falls in sympathy with changes in the level of selling activity. As with production activity, some unit of measure has to be established for selling activity eg £ of sales invoiced or number or physical units invoiced. The normal accounting entries would be:

    (a) Variable Selling Overhead Control A/c   Dr
        Bank A/c   Cr
         or
        Creditors' Control A/c   Cr

Then separately,

(b) Cost of Sales A/c   Dr
      Variable Selling Overhead Control A/c   Cr
        or
      Variable Selling Overhead Applied A/c   Cr
Work-in-Progress Control A/c should not, of course, be debited with this type of expense. There is again a need for a subsidiary ledger at (a).

(8) *FIXED SELLING OVERHEAD*

Emanates from the same analyses as at (7) above. Such expense is regarded as insensitive to rises and falls in selling activity. The normal accounting entries would be:

(a) Fixed Selling Overhead Control A/c Dr   Then separately,
    Bank A/c   Cr (b) Cost of Sales A/c   Dr
    or   Fixed Selling Overhead Control A/c Cr
    Creditors' Control A/c   Cr

There is the usual need for a subsidiary ledger at (a).

TYPICAL QUESTIONS

Question 1
(Adapted from an examination question of The Institute of Chartered Accountants of Scotland.) A light engineering company engaged in the manufacture of a consumer product has produced the following trading and profit and loss account for the year ended 31 July 1978:

	£	£		£	£
Stock as at 1/8/77:			Sales		1,155,000
Raw materials:			Stock as at 31/7/78:		
Dept A	25,500		Raw materials:		
Dept B	3,750		Dept A	21,000	
			Dept B	4,500	
	29,250				
Finished goods	16,020			25,500	
		45,270	Finished goods	18,750	
					44,250
Purchases of raw materials:					
Dept A	345,000				
Dept B	30,000				
		375,000			
Wages:					
Dept A	225,000				
Dept B	300,000				
		525,000			
Power		18,000			
Heat and Light		1,600			
Machine depreciation		10,875			
Loose hand tools		1,530			
Maintenance and repairs:					
Buildings	2,520				
Machinery	3,720				
		6,240			
Rent		13,500			
General Office expenses		24,810			
Administration salaries		30,000			
Advertising		7,500			
Sales, salaries and commission		13,500			
Delivery charges		71,400			
Overdraft interest		1,350			
Profit before taxation		53,675			
		1,199,250			1,199,250

The following additional information has been ascertained:

1. The company has two works departments:
    Dept A – machining of purchased castings
    Dept B – hand assembly of products

2. Of the raw materials used in Dept A 5% are indirect and in Dept B only 40% of the materials used are direct.

3. The hours worked during the year ended 31st July 1978 were:
    Dept A   150,000 machine hours
    Dept B   180,000 direct labour hours

4. The areas occupied by the two works departments and the general office were:
    Dept A   40,000 sq ft
    Dept B   50,000 sq ft
    General Office   10,000 sq ft

5. Of the total wages for each department, the indirect proportion was:
    Dept A   20%
    Dept B   25%

6. Finished goods are valued on a basis including all works costs and administration overhead.

REQUIRED

Re-draft the trading and profit and loss account for the year ended 31 July 1978 in such form as will show the following information:

1. Rates of overhead experienced by the works department to the nearest new penny;

2. Rate of administration overhead expressed as a percentage of works cost of all production to the nearest first decimal place;

3. Rate of selling overhead expressed as a percentage of sales.

Solution
(Issued by kind permission of The Institute of Chartered Accountants of Scotland, who receive contributed solutions from persons whose views are not intended to represent an official Institute opinion.)

See pages 40 and 41.

**Trading and Profit and Loss Account
for the year ended 31 July, 1978**

Line Ref.		£	£	£	£
1	*Sales*				1,155,000
2	*Cost:*				
3	1. Direct Materials – A		332,025		
4	Direct Materials – B		11,700		
5				343,725	
	(Note 1)				
6	2. Direct Labour – A		180,000		
7	Direct Labour – B		225,000		
8				405,000	
	(Note 2)				
9	3. Works Overhead	A	B		
10	Indirect materials	17,475	17,550		
11	Indirect labour	45,000	75,000		
12	Power	18,000	—		
13	Heat and Light (Note 3)	640	800		
14	Machine depreciation	10,875	—		
15	Loose hand tools	—	1,530		
16	Maintenance and repairs:				
17	– buildings (Note 3)	1,008	1,260		
18	– machinery	3,720	—		
19	Rent	5,400	6,750		
20		102,118	102,890		
21				205,008	
22	Production Activity	150,000 *	180,000†		
23	Rate per unit of activity	68p	57p		
24	*Total works cost of current production*			953,733	
25	Add:				
26	*Administration Overhead:*				
27	Heat and light		160		
28	Maintenance and repairs – Buildings		252		
29	Rent		1,350		
30	General office expenses		24,810		
31	Administration salaries		30,000		
32	Overdraft interest		1,350		
33	(6·1% of works cost)			57,922	
34				1,011,655	
35	Add: Opening Finished Goods Stock			16,020	
36	Total available for sale			1,027,675	
37	*Less:* Closing Finished Goods Stock			18,750	
38	*Total works and administration cost of sales*			1,008,925	
39	Add:				
40	*Selling Overhead:*				
41	Advertising		7,500		
42	Sales salaries and commission		13,500		
43		C/F	21,000	1,008,925	1,155,000

* = (machine hours)   † = (direct labour hours)

Trading and Profit and Loss Account (continued)

Line Ref.				£	£	£
1			B/F	21,000	1,008,925	1,155,000
2	Delivery charges			71,400		
3	(8% of Sales)				92,400	
4	*Cost of Sales*					1,101,325
5	*Profit before Tax*					£ 53,675

Line Ref.	6 *Note 1 Stores Account*						
7		Dr	A	B	Cr	A	B
8	Opening Balance		25,500	3,750	To W in P	332,025	11,700
9	Purchases		345,000	30,000	To O'head Control	17,475	17,550
10						349,500	29,250
11					Closing Balance	21,000	4,500
12			370,500	33,750		370,500	33,750

Line Ref.	13 *Note 2 Wages Control*						
14		Dr	A	B	Cr	A	B
15	Total Wages		225,000	300,000	W in P	180,000	225,000
16					Overhead Control	45,000	75,000
17			225,000	300,000		225,000	300,000

Line Ref.	18 *Note 3 Allocations of Overheads*	Heat & Light	Maintenance and repairs – Outbuildings	Rent
19	Dept A 40%	640	1,008	5,400
20	Dept B 50%	800	1,260	6,750
21	Admin 10%	160	252	1,350
22		£1,600	£2,520	£13,500
23	(based on area occupied)			

Question 2

Company X produces 100 machines in period 3. Opening stock is nil. Direct materials total £70,000, direct labour £50,000 and total factory overheads £75,000. Closing stock unsold is 20 machines. Selling price of each machine is £2,200.

REQUIRED

Prepare two statements to show profit for the period: (1) assuming all factory overhead has been incurred in bringing finished machines to completion throughout the year; (2) assuming a factory overhead recovery rate of £250 per machine.

Solution

Company X

Profit Statement for Period 3

	Alternative statements			
	1		*2*	
	Units	£	Units	£
Sales	80	176,000	80	176,000
Cost of Current Production	100		100	
Direct Materials		70,000		70,000
Direct Labour		50,000		50,000
Factory Overheads		75,000		75,000
Total costs of current production	100	195,000	100	195,000
Add: opening stock	—	—	—	—

		100	195,000	100	195,000
Less: closing stock (Note 1)		20	39,000	20	29,000
Cost of sales		80	156,000	80	166,000
Profit for period		80	20,000	80	10,000

Note 1   Valuation of closing stock:

$$\text{Statement 1: } 20 \times \frac{195,000}{100} = \text{£}39,000$$

$$\text{Statement 2: } 20 \times \frac{70,000 + 50,000}{100} + 20 \times \text{£}250$$

$$= \text{£}29,000$$

Question 3

A factory uses an application rate of £4 per unit of production activity. Actual overhead costs of £3,600 are under-applied by £200. What is the level of production in units?

Solution
The overhead applied must have been £3,600 less £200 = £3,400. If the rate of application (or absorption) was £4 per unit, the production level must have been £3,400 ÷ 4 = 850 units.

Question 4

What bases for apportionment would you consider fair for transferring the following service department costs?
     1. Power house   2. Tool room   3. Canteen

Solution
Power house: costs incurred in providing and maintaining the power house, such as depreciation and wages could be apportioned to users in proportion to respective numbers of units of budgeted usage (a total charge to each customer for the period), whereas variable operating costs such as fuel could be apportioned according to actual usage. Where possible, meters would measure usage of units of power consumed by each customer department. Where meter measurement was not possible, the total working hours for all customer departments × the total horse-power of the machines in use could be used to derive an activity denominator: this would be divided into the total variable operating costs to obtain a charging rate. Each user department would then be charged at this rate × number of hours worked × horse-power of machinery.
Tool room: many tool room costs are incurred in anticipation of possible usage or demand rather than actual demand. Usage or demand can be expressed in several ways, eg (1) number of requisitions, (2) value of requisitions, or (3) through a formula which weights value of issues and number of requisitions. As with power house costs, each user department may be charged a lump sum for the period plus extra at a rate based on one of (1) to (3) above. Many firms apportion (charge out) total tool room running costs to each customer department in proportion to normal or expected usage. It should be noted that details of tool usage are normally shown on requisitions, so that tool costs can be charged directly to the departments concerned; the question is concerned with the charging of the costs of running the tool room.
Canteen: frequency of usage by employees is seldom analysed by department. Total canteen costs (when a canteen is wholly subsidised) or the canteen deficit (when partly subsidised) are usually apportioned to user departments on the basis of normal, or average, or budgeted head-count for each department.

5 Profit Centre Reporting and Transfer Pricing

Profit Centres

The Institute of Cost and Management Accountants has defined a 'profit centre' as 'a division of an organisation to which both expenditure and revenue are attributable and in respect of which profitability can be assessed'. (Terminology, 3.224)

In practice, however, the profits of an organisation may be split (or segmented) in many ways which are certainly not mutually exclusive. For example, a large professional accountancy firm might segment overall profits by:

(a) office location
(b) manager
(c) division (auditing, taxation, liquidations, etc)
(d) customer
(e) customer category (sole traders, limited companies, local authorities, government departments, etc.)

The purposes of segmentation of profits include:

(1) determination of whether the objectives of separate parts of an organisation are in fact being achieved. If total profits are not analysed, success or failure of various segments to achieve their own particular objectives will not be revealed.

(2) disclosure of areas of rapid growth, and, conversely, of decline, so that additional resources may be provided to underpin areas which should have support, with 'expiring' activities being deprived of resources which they cannot effectively utilise.

(3) measuring of management performance, so that additional responsibilities may be offered to those with good performance records.

(4) identification of separate categories of risk. For example, a company might decide to segment overall profits into 'home' and 'export' operations, to determine how dependent it was upon overseas trading. Another might analyse profits to determine degrees of dependence upon, say, customers in (a) the car industry, (b) the steel industry and (c) the domestic appliance industry. A third might segment profits to show, separately, the proportions emanating from (a) the electronics industry (b) the music industry (c) the entertainment industry and (d) the food industry. This latter company might well have several subsidiary companies and/or divisions belonging to each industry type: these would be drawn together to form total impressions under each of the above four headings.

Profit centre reporting can be expected to exist in profusion, with management support, and to show a true and fair view, when there is:

(1) A minimum of internal trading between segments, and thus a minimum of transfer pricing.

(2) A maximum of trading by each segment with external (third) parties.

(3) A minimum of communal (shared) costs.

(4) A minimum of 'shielding' of profit centres from tribulations which would cause damage were these segments to be trading on their own.

(5) A minimum of difficulty in apportioning capital employed.

Item (3) can be expected when profit centres are geographically separated. The shielding referred to at (4) would include cases where a profit centre was able to bail itself out of a liquidity crisis by borrowing cash from another profit centre, or to borrow resources such as staff to enable it to make profits often at the expense of the profit centre(s) temporarily deprived of these resources. Again, a particular profit centre might be able to share, say, office facilities with a stronger profit centre; for example, a struggling new consultancy department of a professional accountancy firm would be able to avoid the costs of its own commissionaire, receptionist, typing pool and switchboard operator if it could be located in the same building as well-established auditing and taxation departments.

There are three basic ways in which profit centre results can be derived:

(1) Sales less full costs (variable and fixed) = profit.
(2) Sales less (variable costs plus *direct* fixed costs) = contribution to general (establishment) fixed costs.
(3) Sales less variable costs only = contribution to total fixed costs.

If the professional accountancy firm referred to above had a computer which provided information only to the consultancy department, its rental and other operating fixed costs could be classed as *direct* fixed costs to the consultancy profit centre. However, if the computer aided 'all and sundry' throughout the firm, a decision might be taken not to try to apportion computer fixed costs across each profit centre: the firm might then choose to determine comparative *contributions* in line with level (3) above.

In general, profit centre reporting may be:

(1) occasional

(2) carried out in many different ways within the same time period

(3) approximate, to provide impressions rather than precise results

It should always be based on reliable basic documentation. The choice of profit centre type used should only be made after receiving answers to the following questions: does the proposed profit centre type

(1) create problems as regards transfer pricing?

(2) involve an excess of arbitrary guesswork on the splitting of communal (fixed) costs?

(3) make trend analysis and comparison virtually impossible because profit centres will constantly change their sizes, compositions and purposes over the years?

(4) fulfil useful purposes regarding future decision making?

(5) require the implementation of new account coding procedures, or is it based on already existing and reliable coding operations?

(6) form the basis for true and fair views of segmental performance, or are there likely to be hidden, intangible influences which will not show up on monetary performance reports?

(7) hold the prospect of too much or too little internal competitiveness among staff, with the possibility of a conflict of interest among profit centres?

(8) lend itself to reliable splitting of capital employed?

Transfer Pricing

For the purposes of this text, transfer pricing is restricted to transfers between profit centres. The major methods used include:

(1) full cost

(2) market price

(3) negotiated price

The choice of method depends entirely upon circumstances.

Full cost appears to be simple and easily understood, yet the management accountant will realise that 'full cost' frequently contains apportioned fixed costs which have been divided on the basis of sheer guesswork and/or subjective opinions on what constitutes fair play.

The transferor makes no profit, and should ostensibly have a grievance, *yet* he may well be relieved if at the time of transfer he was suffering from under-utilisation of capacity and facing the prospect of under-recovery of fixed costs. If the proportion of transferor's sales to total sales which comprise internal transfers is volatile, any trend on the transferor's performance may be damaged. In a particular year, for example, he may make a profit on virtually all sales because they happen to be to outsiders, whereas in another very few sales may be 'profit-loaded' as they largely comprise sales to other profit centres in his organisation.

'Full cost' may contain the results of inefficiency, so that there may be little incentive to the transferor to control costs. The converse is also true, in that the transferor must pass on any benefits from efficiency in a lower transfer price.

Market price may not be known if the intermediate goods are not in a saleable condition. In addition, the goods (or services) offered may be so specialised that market price can only be the subject of guesswork.

Clearly the transferor scores when using this method, and has considerable incentive to trade with other profit centres. In periods of recession, an otherwise bad trading performance of the transferor can be turned into a success story if the transferee is known to be 'rescuing' the transferor. In any event, a fairer method might be to discount the market price if the transferee is providing constancy and certainty of demand to the transferor, as these factors are likely to result in cost savings to the latter.

Negotiated price is usually based on market price, with a discount being allowed to the transferee as a result of benefits accruing to the transferor from trading internally rather than with third parties. For example, marketing and advertising costs may be partly avoided, and production and distribution scheduling can be arranged well in advance to suit both parties and minimise costs. However the exact amount of any discount may be open to negotiation, and the eventual outcome of 'management talks' may not have the full support of all interested parties. Performance trends of both sides of a transfer transaction will always be slightly distorted when the percentage of internal sales/purchases to total sales/purchases is volatile, but the distortion will never be very substantial.

Whenever transfer pricing is in use, two important criteria emerge:

(1) the need to maximise 'goal congruence'.
(2) the need to recognise 'opportunity cost'.

If a professional accountancy firm were to transfer a member of the London audit department to the Bristol audit department, transfer pricing might be necessary if each were a profit centre. If 'full cost' were used, goal congruence would arise if the managers of each centre acquiesced without any feelings of grievance, and relished further transactions of a similar kind in the future. Such feelings of empathy between transferor and transferee might arise if the London office had no work to which their audit staff member could charge time, and the Bristol office would otherwise have been unable to serve a client's needs. Goal congruence might well be lost, if, on the other hand, the London office manager discovered that London's full cost was, say £7 per hour, and Bristol's full cost for their own establishment staff was, say, £10 per hour. London might then consider that they were merely being used as an 'employment agency' from which more and more skilled staff might be called off to the transferor's trading detriment.

If, in the above case, full cost was assessed at, say, £9 per hour and market price at say, £12, an *opportunity cost* of £3 per hour would be lost if London were obliged to route saleable hours away from their own clients, from whom £12 would be obtained, to Bristol office, who would pay £9. Bristol might then be tempted to under-charge their clients in an effort to become more competitive, charging, say, £11 per hour. In this way the cash inflow to the firm as a whole might only be £11. Consequently, many organisations absorb opportunity costs fully into transfer prices, so that as much pressure as possible is brought to bear on profit centres 'at the sharp end' of the business, to achieve high levels of cash inflow if they are to be regarded as profitable.

6 Standard Costing

There can be no doubt that the ultimate discipline in business is a comparison of overall total performance against budget for a period. But standard costing is invaluable in relating overall budgets to more minute circumstances, narrowing concentration to the elements which need attention at individual transaction level; the cost per unit of a raw material part, the throughput in units per hour of a particular machine, the oil consumption per hour of a particular boiler, and so on. Any degree of deviation from expectation or standard for each of the above items, triggers off a variance which may well have a bearing on the ultimate achievement of a budget. At this level, variances can be pinned down to specific causes and to specific people for attention.

Caveats

If a wide range of products exists, the preparation of standards can be very lengthy, as a standard product cost sheet should be prepared for every product, covering all the constituent parts of cost (direct materials, direct wages, variable overheads and fixed overheads). By like token the revision of standards can also be very time consuming, but in times of economic difficulties, changing product specifications and designs, material shortages and inflation, the need for revision of standards at regular intervals is urgent. The use of standard costing implies that stock is valued at a standard or estimated cost. Should there be delay in comparing standards with actual costs, all or some of that stock will presumably be sold, and the appropriate 'snowball' of standard cost transferred to a cost of sales account. Slow reaction to the need for comparison can therefore result in failure to recover sufficient cost from customers, especially in times of inflation. In many cases a variance analysis may reveal too late that standards are well below actual costs, and that the products which were responsible for the variances have been sold, leaving management with no choice but to treat the variances as period costs. They can, after all, only be regarded as product costs if the relevant products are still in stock.

Stock Valuations at Standard Cost

In balance sheet terms, the assets which a company using standard costing will hold 'at standard cost' are Raw Material Stocks, Work-in-Progress Stocks, and Finished Goods Stocks. If deviations between these standard valuations and actual costs are insignificant, auditors will probably allow the company concerned to use the standard valuations on its actual balance sheet. To make things simple, let us suppose that 100 units of raw materials are purchased which ought to have cost £1 each (ie having a standard cost of £1 each). Suppose actual cost is £1·50 per unit. The company's trial balance will show:

	Dr	Cr
Stock (at Standard)	100	
Raw Material/Price variance	50	
Bank (overdraft)		150
	£150	£150

Accounting practice would require an adjustment to the stock valuation prior to finalisation of the balance sheet. This would be done by journal entry.

Stock	Dr	£50
Price Variance	Cr	£50

The nominal ledger balances for balance sheet purposes would then be:

	Dr	Cr
Stock	150	
Bank (overdraft)		150
Profit and Loss Account	—	—
	150	£150

However, if the company could show that the standard costs were dependable and that the purchase at £1·50 was a dreadful mistake, the auditors of the company might well agree to leave the variance at £50 and carry foward stock at a standard value of £100 after all, especially if the company's selling prices of ultimate finished goods had been set to recover only £100.

In standard costing terms, a variance shows the extent to which a standard cost evaluation is greater than, or less than, the actual cost incurred. As is implied in the simple example above, variances tend to be given full nominal ledger status in their own right. Debit variances on a trial balance are regarded as unfavourable, in that they give evidence that, when all is said and done, some cash payment at some time has exceeded what was expected (standard). Debit variances are really 'stock assets in disguise'. They represent the extent that a standard stock value elsewhere on the trial balance has fallen short of reality in terms of cost. Credit balances represent favourable variances in that they show the extent to which standard stock valuations elsewhere on the trial balance overstate actual costs.

When debit and credit variance balances are immaterial, or are caused by problems which should not be allowed to infiltrate standard closing stock valuations, they are closed out by journal entry and transferred to the debit of Profit and Loss Account (unfavourable variances) or the credit of Profit and Loss Account (favourable variances). Thus, in the simple example above, the balance sheet position would show:

Sources of Funds		£
Bank overdraft		150

Uses of funds		
Stock (at standard)	100	
Profit and loss deficit	50	
	—	150

Note the contrast with the nominal ledger balances on the previous page.

There are, however, certain variances which should not be considered as assets in disguise and transferred to stock accounts as late amendments to faulty standard evaluations. In other words, there are certain deviations from plans which unsold products should not be saddled with. Firstly, each product should have attached to it only a fair and equitable portion of manufacturing fixed expense. If fewer products are made than expected each should still have only this same fair portion. The under-recovery of fixed expense caused by lack of activity (known as a fixed overhead volume variance) should be regarded as a period charge. Supposing manufacturing fixed expenses for a period are budgeted at £10,000 and production is anticipated as 10,000 units. The standard fixed overhead recovery rate will then be £1 for each unit made. We may be talking here about the situation in a department or in a factory as a whole. Thus, if these 10,000 are made as planned, but unsold, each will carry £1 as part of its cost, to cover manufacturing fixed expense. If, however, only 5,000 are made and remain unsold, each should still carry £1 of manufacturing fixed expense, and *not* £10,000 ÷ 5,000 = £2. If each carries only £1, a further £5,000 remains to be accounted for, and this is 'orphan' cost with no products to which to belong. As a result a variance of £10,000–£5,000 arises which becomes cost to be charged immediately to the period in which the lack of production activity took place. The situation in trial balance terms would be (assuming actual fixed costs incurred are £10,000).

	Dr £	Cr £
Stock at Standard (fixed overhead portion only) .	5,000	
Profit and Loss Account (after transfer from a Fixed Overhead Volume Variance Account)	5,000	
Bank Overdraft		10,000
	10,000	10,000

Standard Product Cost excludes Abnormal Scrap

Another type of variance which does not belong as product cost is an abnormal scrap variance. Most standard costs used allow for normal scrap; for example, the cost of making 10 units might need to be borne by 9 good units, one unit failing at inspection. The effect of making good production bear the cost of making a reasonable amount of spoilt production is to regard normal spoilage or waste just as much a manufacturing cost as wages or overheads such as heat, light and power. If, in the above illustration, 10 units were made but only 8 passed inspection, the normal scrap situation would not then have arisen. Nevertheless the 8 good units would each still carry the same burden of spoilage or scrap expense as each of the 9 would have carried. If the standard cost of making 10 was £27, the valuation of 9 good units would be

$$\frac{£27 \text{ (cost of making 10)}}{10-10\% \text{ normal scrap}} = £3 \text{ each.}$$

Total recovery of cost against good production would be $9 \times £3 = £27$.

However, the valuation of 8 good units would still be at the rate of: $\dfrac{£27 \text{ (cost of making 10)}}{10-10\% \text{ normal scrap}} = £3$

each. The total recovery of cost would be $8 \times £3 = £24$ as product cost, plus $£27 - £24 = £3$ abnormal scrap variance chargeable as period cost against the performance of those responsible for the abnormal spoilage. The trial balance situation would be:

	Dr £	Cr £
Stock at Standard (8 units)	24	
Profit and loss account	3	
Bank overdraft		27
	27	27

If 9 units were made, the situation would be:

	Dr	Cr
Stock at Standard	27	
Bank overdraft		27

Acceptable Cash Outgoings are Replaced by Stock Increases

A key objective of standard costing is to establish a cost recovery mechanism whereby 'CASH MINUS' sums are converted 'pound for pound' to 'STOCK PLUS', in a balance sheet environment. Pricing policies for finished goods are often dependent upon the reliability of standard costing. Standard stock figures become COST OF SALES amounts in due course, and the latter have to be 'topped' by SALES amounts if a company is to survive. The 'cost of sales at standard' balance appears as a debit on the trial balance: if there are also debit balances appearing on the trial balance from variance accounts, these will show the extent to which actual costs incurred have not been reflected in the 'cost of sales at standard' figure. In such cases it is to be hoped that (1) the basis for prices charged was standard cost of sales *plus* adverse variances ie that the adverse variances were identified in time and/or (2) there are significant credit (favourable) variances which might counter-balance any problems caused by adverse variances.

Variances Show Profit Deviations

Every variance which has full nominal ledger and trial balance status should be able to support the prefix 'profit variance caused by . . .'. In the context of standard costing, 'variance' relates to the difference between actual profit as shown on the balance sheet as 'Profit and Loss Account balance' and the profit *expected* to appear there. Consider the following simplified example:

ABC Ltd have budgeted to produce and sell 1,000 units of product A, at a standard cost of £6 per unit and a selling price of £7. The standard cost comprises £2 for direct materials, £2 for direct labour, 50p to recover variable overheads and £1·50 to absorb fixed overheads. In practice, 800 units are produced and sold; actual direct material costs are £1,700, direct labour £1,750, variable overheads £480 and fixed overheads £1,450. Actual selling price per unit is £7·50.

Required: prepare a performance statement comparing actual with budgeted results.

Solution

ABC Ltd: Performance Statement (Period   –   )

Line Ref.		Budget Units	Budget £	Actual Units	Actual £
1	Sales at standard prices	1,000	7,000	800	5,600
2	*Less:* cost of sales at standard	1,000		800	
3	Direct materials		2,000		1,600
4	Direct labour		2,000		1,600
5	Variable overheads		500		400
6	Fixed overheads		1,500		1,200
7	Total		6,000		4,800
8	*Budgeted profit*		1,000		
9	Standard profit on actual sales . . . . *Add:*				800
10	Sales price variance (Note 1) . . . . *Less:*		400		400
11	Sales volume variance (Note 2)		(200)		
12			1,200		1,200
	Less: unfavourable cost variances				
13	Direct materials				(100)
14	Direct labour				(150)
15	Variable overheads				(80)
16	Fixed overhead volume . . . . *Add:* favourable cost variance				(300)
17	Fixed overhead expenditure				50
18	Actual profit				620

The company set out to make £1,000 profit and actually made £620. The total unfavourable profit variance is £380.

If we relate the situation to the balance sheets (budgeted and actual), the difference of £380 is again highlighted. [Suppose sales are not paid for, and that all expenses have been paid in cash.]

Balance Sheet

	Budget £	Actual £	Difference £
Sources of Funds			
Bank overdraft	6,000	5,380	620
Profit and Loss Account	1,000	620	380
	7,000	6,000	1,000
Employment of Funds			
Debtors	7,000	6,000	1,000

You can see the profit variance of £380 above. Standard costing relates actual profit to expected profit, and details reasons for any upsurge or disappointment, so that individual managers can be asked to take action which will accentuate strengths and make them routine, and eliminate unexpected weaknesses. Each variance has a title which gives clear pointers towards its cause.

Note 1 (See line reference 10)

Sales price variance = act. qty. sold × standard selling price

v

act. qty. sold × actual selling price

[800 × £7 v 800 × 7·50 = £400 (Favourable)]

Note 2 (See line reference 11)

Sales volume variance = budgeted sales qty. × standard unit profit

v

actual sales qty. × standard unit profit

[1,000 × £1 v 800 × £1 = £200 (Unfavourable)]

Standard costing performance reports, sometimes known as operating statements, should open with standard sales values and standard costs being 'given their chance' to show what profit *ought* to be. Variances are then listed, showing the extent to which standard profit is at variance with the real facts. Line 9 on the preceding report layout shows management the profit which they had every right to expect at the actual production and sales level of 800 units. Lines 10 and 11 show the extent to which the selling function has influenced events by (a) changing selling prices and (b) selling a quantity differing from plan. As a result of (a) and (b), the actual profit has (a) risen by £400, and (b) declined by £200 respectively against budgeted profit. After line 12, the sales function's representatives can be asked to return to their desks, and production management are asked to deliberate upon the remaining variance lines, which show the extent to which the figures in the actual column, at lines 3 to 6, did not take place because of faulty crystal ball gazing or deviations in efficiency or activity.

The above layout can be re-designed, giving the same information in a different format, *see opposite page*. At line 6, fixed costs are *not* being flexed. It is the standard stock valuation which is being adjusted (or flexed) away from the valuation of budgeted quantities of production to the valuation of actual quantities. 200 fewer units were made; therefore the stock on the shelves (col (3) quantities) is worth £300 less in terms of fixed standard value. It is *because* fixed costs will remain fixed despite production level changes that the £300 is taken as an adverse profit variance at col (5)(e). Cash can still be expected to drop by £1,500 even although stock valuation only

Line Ref.		(1) Original budget		(2) Flexing to allow for activity change		(3) Revised standard sales/charges to cost		(4) Actual Activity and costs		(5) Variances affecting profits					
										(a) Sales Price £	(b) Sales Volume £	(c) Cost £	(d) Exp.† £	(e) F/O'head Volume £	(f) Total £
		Units	£	Units	£	Units	£	Units	£						
1	Sales	1,000	7,000	200	1,400	800	5,600	800	6,000	400(F)					400(F)
2	Cost of Sales	1,000		200		800		800							
3	Direct materials		2,000		400		1,600		1,700			100(U)			100(U)
4	Direct labour		2,000		400		1,600		1,750			150(U)			150(U)
5	Variable overheads		500		100		400		480			80(U)			80(U)
6	Fixed overheads		1,500		300		1,200		1,450				50(F)	300(U)	250(U)
7	Total	1,000	6,000	200	1,200	800	4,800	800	5,380						
8	Profit	1,000	1,000	200*	200*	800	800	800	620		200*(U)				200(U)
9	Variances									400(F)	200(U)	330(U)	50(F)	300(U)	380(U)
										(a)	(b)	(c)	(d)	(e)	(f)

The total at column 5 (f) shows the aggregate shortfall of actual profit (£620) against the original profit of £1,000. Each time this format is used, the total of column (2) forms the sales volume variance, ie the increase (or decrease) in profits caused by selling more (or less) than budgeted.

†Column 5(d) shows the fixed production overhead expenditure variance, which is defined in 'The Terminology of Management and Financial Accountancy' as 'the difference between the budget cost allowance for production for a specified control period and the amount of actual fixed expenditure attributed and charged to that period.' Full titles and definitions of all variances dealt with in this book are provided in the 'Terminology', which is published by The Institute of Cost and Management Accountants.

shows £1,200! In this example, the situation has been slightly alleviated in that the actual expense turned out to be £1,450, so that the Balance Sheet stock valuation (for fixed cost content) is £1,200, for a 'CASH MINUS' of £1,450. The difference of £250 (unfavourable) is shown at (5)(f) and is the charge to Profit and Loss Account.

Balance Sheet [as affected by Fixed Costs]

	Budget £	Actual £
Application of Funds		
Stock 1,000 × 1·50	1,500	
800 × 1·50		1,200
	═══	═══
Source of Funds		
Overdraft	1,500	1,450
Profit & Loss Account (loss)	—	(250)
	═══	═══

(Profit difference (or variance) £250)

The management of many companies would welcome the presentation of the above performance statement in a single column format, provided variances between actual and budgeted results were still included and laid out in a logical sequence. The following layout should cater for those who prefer the simpler, single column approach:

ABC Ltd: Performance Statement (Period————)

	£
Budgeted sales at standard selling prices	7,000
Less: budgeted cost of sales at standard	6,000
	———
Budgeted profit	1,000
Less: unfavourable sales volume variance	200
	———
Standard profit on actual sales	800
Add: favourable sales price variance	400
	———
Standard profit, actual quantities, actual selling prices, standard costs . .	1,200
Add/(deduct): favourable/(unfavourable) cost variances	
Direct materials	(100)
Direct labour	(150)
Variable overheads	(80)
Fixed overhead volume	(300)
Fixed overhead expenditure	50
	———
Actual profit	£620
	═══

When a single column layout is used, the management accountant should reflect as much planning effort as possible on the top line, eg '*budgeted* sales at *standard* selling prices'. Those who have taken the trouble to prepare standards and budgets should have their fleeting moment in the spotlight. The two words in italics above trigger off variances further down the statement, viz the sales volume variance and the sales price variance. If there is a shortage of information about original plans, an alternative top line becomes necessary eg: (1) 'sales at standard selling prices', when only actual quantities sold are known and (2) 'actual sales', when neither original sales quantities nor original selling prices are known. The situation at (1) means that any presentation of a sales volume variance must drop out. At (2), both the sales volume variance and the sales price variance are not attainable and cannot be provided on a statement.

Controllable and Non-Controllable Variances

Standard costing systems are set up so that each variance produced can be related to specific individuals for appraisal, and, if the variance is considered *controllable*, for action. Each variance has a cause. Some of these causes are controllable, and others uncontrollable in that external factors are responsible, such as closure of suppliers' premises, Government action, etc.

Offsetting Variances Stemming from same Decision

Standard costing quantifies the monetary effect of unexpected events, so that a balanced view on remedial action can be taken. Two variances may be set off against each other as emanating from the common root source of a single management decision. For example, a decision to buy raw materials from an alternative supplier could result in an adverse price variance of, say, £100, but the materials could prove easier to process with less wastage, with a consequent favourable material usage variance of £300. This would give a net favourable variance of £200 and could well vindicate the decision to change suppliers. The same type of comparison can be made when dealing with other elements of cost, for example between adverse direct labour rate variances (using more expensive grades of labour than planned) and favourable direct labour efficiency variances (fewer hours taken than expected to complete the work in hand). In any event prompt reporting of variances provides a springboard for future action either to rectify problems or to follow up some unexpected advantage.

Difficulties in Setting Up a Standard Costing System

There are of course difficulties in setting up a standard costing system. Disregarded, they could cause sophisticated variance accounting schemes simply to go out like candles.

Standard costing systems can be very expensive both to set up and to operate, so that cost justification becomes a prime difficulty. In some companies, the advocates of standard costing are required to 'spell out' net cost savings which could be expected to emanate from the system.

It becomes essential to canvass support from as wide a range of managers as possible, to spread the setting up cost over a variety of functions, departments and locations likely to benefit from increased productivity, improved efficiency and cost control emanating after system start-up.

Setting up costs require to be approved at budget time and attributed to the costs of individual managers and this is a sensitive area. Of greater concern, however, would be attempts to charge actual costs of setting up the system when no costs had been budgeted, causing substantial adverse variances.

The distinctions between controllable and non-controllable variances should be attempted while the system is still at the design stage: these distinctions are not easy to make unless related firstly to controllable and non-controllable *costs*. Managers are more inclined to discuss controllability of costs than responsibility for creating and then taking blame for variances. Many variances are initially listed as non-controllable and considerable persuasion has to be brought to bear on individual managers before agreement is reached that they are in fact controllable.

The optimum degree of detailed variance analysis is difficult to establish, and many mistakes can be made unless simulation tests are carried out at the systems design stage, or even earlier – at the feasibility stage – to test the value of proposed variances to users. If a demanding, precise level of detail is called for, in due course various unjustified assumptions may need to be made on an ongoing basis to force transaction data into over-detailed categories. On the other hand, aggregate variances which in themselves fail to answer management queries lead to time-consuming 'ad-hoc' enquiries, sometimes with manual transaction record analysis, to expose required levels of detail.

If no standard costing system has previously been in use, there will usually be a serious lack of detail at product/process/job level, on which to base standard product specification sheet information. There will be the temptation to make guesses, particularly if the introduction of the system is running to tight deadlines.

Measurements of performance, which form the basis for standards, should be made under normal operating conditions, but these may be difficult both to obtain and to identify in the first place. This problem can be aggravated when accountants and systems analysts advocating standard costing lack knowledge and experience of the company and its processes, either because they are new employees or because they lack previous exposure to operating conditions.

There is an accounting burden in preparing standard cost specification sheets prior to start-up, for no immediate benefit. This work-load has to be placed at a sensible point on the calendar, and manpower found to achieve it within deadlines.

There is the constant need to estimate: standards are estimates. This involves determining future practical capacity levels, planned usage of practical capacity and scrap levels, as well as cost levels. The timing and frequency of output reports has to be agreed in advance. Output times are of course affected by delays to data input. The speed of output reports to manager X may often depend on the speed of data input to the system from manager Y. Friction can emanate from differing output reporting date requirements among potential management users.

Finally, in some companies conditions change rapidly and in addition no two products or jobs may be exactly alike. There is a danger in attempting to classify differing production activity as standard for the sake of the system.

Practice on Central Themes

At this stage the central theme of standard costing, the preparation of performance statements comparing actual with budgeted results, should be consolidated through the use of two sample questions which the reader might care to use for practising purposes before studying the solutions which are reproduced immediately after each. No apology need be made for such little tests as they reassure the reader that his progress is steady.

TYPICAL QUESTIONS

Question 1
Alpha Beta Gamma Ltd is affected by a recession in the industry to which it belongs. Various levels of production activity are shown below:

(1) Previous year's level of activity	*For std recovery rates of fixed cost + oHAS*	10,000 units
(2) 'Normal' level of activity		12,000 units
(3) Current year's budgeted level of activity		8,000 units
(4) Current year's actual level of activity		6,000 units

The current year's budgeted and actual fixed production costs are £48,000 and £50,000 respectively. Variable production costs for the current year are £1 per unit (standard cost) and £1·05 per unit (actual cost). Budgeted and actual fixed administration overheads are £15,000 and £16,000 respectively. The budgeted selling price per unit is £8, and the actual unit price attained is £7.

Required: prepare a profit and loss account comparing actual with budgeted results, on the basis that half of the current production activity has been sold, the balance remaining as closing stock. Value closing stock to include fixed and variable production cost elements, and also administration. Show units columns as well as monetary columns. There is no opening stock on hand. Ignore selling expenses.

Solution

Profit and Loss Account

Line Ref.		Budget Units	Budget £	Actual Units	Actual £
1	Sales at standard selling prices	8,000	64,000	3,000 @ 8	24,000
2	Current production and administration:				*at std.*
3	costs at standard	8,000		6,000	
4	variable production costs		8,000		6,000 ✓
5	Fixed production costs (Note 1)		48,000		24,000
6	Fixed administration overheads (Note 2) . . .		15,000		7,500
7			71,000		37,500
8	*Less:* closing stock at standard (Note 3)	—	—	3,000	18,750
9	Cost of sales at standard	8,000	71,000	3,000	18,750
10	Budgeted profit/(loss)		(7,000)		
	Standard profit on actual sales				
11	at standard selling prices				5,250
	Add/(deduct)				
12	Unfavourable sales price variance (Note 4) . . .		3,000		(3,000)
	Add/(deduct)				
13	sales volume variance (Note 5)		8,750		
14			(18,750)		
15	*Less:* budgeted fixed cost volume				
16	variances: production (unfav) (Note 6) . .		16,000		
17	administration (unfav) (Note 7) .		5,000		
18			2,250		2,250
19	*Less:* unfavourable cost variances				
20	variable production (Note 8)				(300)
	fixed cost volume variances				
21	– production (Note 9)				(24,000)
22	– administration (Note 10)				(7,500)
	fixed cost expenditure variances				
23	– production (Note 11)				(2,000)
24	– administration (Note 12)				(1,000)
25	Actual profit/(loss) for year				(32,550)

Note 1 The standard recovery rate is based on the 'normal' level of activity of 12,000 units. The rate is:

$$\frac{48,000}{12,000} \text{ units} = £4 \text{ per unit.}$$

Management must deliberately ensure the write off of a heavy burden of fixed costs in the current period; they will have known about this problem at the time of budget preparation. Consequently the sum of £48,000 in the Budget column for fixed production costs is made up of 8,000 × £4 which they would be hoping to recover in stock valuation, plus £16,000 of 'problem cost' which was budgeted but not recoverable = a total expected cost of £48,000. See also Note 9.

Note 2 The standard recovery rate is again based on 12,000 units:

$$\frac{£15,000}{12,000} = £1 \cdot 25.$$

The sum of £15,000 is made up of 8,000 × £1·25 = £12,000 plus £3,000 problem (non-recoverable) cost.

Note 3   Valuation of closing stock must include the three elements included in the question: variable production costs at £1 per unit, fixed production at £4 per unit and admin. overheads at £1·25 per unit: total standard cost per unit = £6·25. The closing stock value is therefore 3,000 × £6·25 = £18,750.

Note 4   Actual quantity × (Standard – actual selling price per unit) = 3,000 × £1 = £3,000 (unfav).

Note 5   (Budgeted – actual) quantity × standard unit profit
= (8,000–3,000) × £8–6·25
= 5,000 × £1·75 = £8,750 (unfav)

Note 6	Fixed production cost	£48,000
	Less:	
	planned production × recovery rate	
	8,000 × £4	£32,000
		£16,000 (unfav)

Note 7	Fixed administration cost	£15,000
	Less:	
	planned production × recovery rate	
	8,000 × £1·25	£10,000
		£5,000 (unfav)

Note 8   6,000 units × £(1–1·05) = £300 (unfav)

Note 9	12,000 × application rate of £4	£48,000
	Less:	
	6,000 × application rate of £4	£24,000
		£24,000 (unfav)

Note 10	12,000 × application rate of £1·25	£15,000
	Less:	
	6,000 × application rate of £1·25	£ 7,500
		£ 7,500 (unfav)

Note 11   £48,000 budget less £50,000 actual = £2,000 (unfav)

Note 12   £15,000 budget less £16,000 actual = £1,000 (unfav)

56

Question 2

ABC Ltd budget to manufacture and sell 100 units in Period 4. Sales prices are expected to be £30 per unit, but in practice customers are charged £3,500 for 110 units actually sold. Production costs are budgeted at £1,000 (variable) and £800 (fixed) for the planned production level of 100 units. Fixed administration cost is expected to be £500 for the period. In practice, the 110 units made cost £1,400 for variable production costs, £900 for fixed production costs and £300 for fixed administration costs. Fixed selling costs are budgeted at £600, but actual expenditure is £700. Full absorption costing is in use. The company operates a system of standard costing and flexible budgetary control.

Required: prepare an operating statement comparing actual with budgeted results, and showing detailed variances.

Solution – two solution formats are set out below.

Presentation Style No. 1

ABC Ltd: Operating Statement: Period 4

	£
Budgeted sales at standard selling prices	3,000
Less: budgeted cost of sales at standard	2,900
Budgeted profit	100
Add: favourable sales volume variance	70
Standard profit on actual sales quantities	170
Add: sales price variance	200
Standard profit, actual quantities, actual selling prices, standard costs	370
Add/(deduct): favourable/(unfavourable) cost variance:	
Variable production cost	(300)
Fixed production expenditure	(100)
Fixed production volume	80
Fixed administration expenditure	200
Fixed administration volume	50
Selling cost expenditure	(100)
Actual profit	£200

At line 7 of presentation style No. 2 (*overleaf*) a decision has been taken not to calculate a selling cost volume variance. Some managers would find such a variance useful: the operating statement would then show 10 units in column (2) at line 7, with £60 in the monetary column (2). Column (3) would show 110 units and £660. The 'knock-on' effect of this would be to reduce the column (2) profit figure from £70 to £10. Thus there would be an additional variance of £60 at column 5(e), the figure in column 5(b) would be reduced to £10(F) and the total at 5(f) would remain unchanged at £100(F). Any decision to provide a fixed selling cost volume variance should be taken after consultation with management as to whether it might be merely an unnecessary complication.

Presentation Style No. 2

ABC Ltd: Operating Statement: Period 4

ABSORPTION COSTING

Line Ref.	(1) Original budget Units	£	(2) Flexing for activity change Units	£	(3) Revised standard sales/charges to production Units	£	(4) Actual Activity/costs Units	£	(5) Variances affecting profits (a) Sales Price	(b) Sales Volume (Col. (2) total)	(c) Selling cost expenditure	(d) Cost or expenditure	(e) Volume	(f) Total
1 Sales	100	3,000	10	300	110	3,300	110	3,500	200(F)					200(F)
2 Production and administration cost of sales	100		10		110		110							
3 Variable production		1,000		100		1,100		1,400				300(U)		300(U)
4 Fixed production		800		80		880		900				100(U)	80(F)	20(U)
5 Fixed administration		500		50		550		300				200(F)	50(F)	250(F)
6 Total production and administration cost of sales	100	2,300	10	230	110	2,530	110	2,600						
7 Selling costs		600	—			600		700			100(U)			100(U)
8 Total cost of sales	100	2,900	10	230	110	3,130	110	3,300		70(F)				70(F)
9 Profit	100	100	10	70	110	170	110	200	200(F)	70(F)	100(U)	200(U)	130(F)	100(F)

Note: Stock is valued at full production and administration cost

(*Note*: Full titles of the variances (a) to (e) above, and definitions in each case, are provided in the 'Terminology of Management and Financial Accountancy' published by The Institute of Cost and Management Accountants.)

Objectives of Standard Costing

As a conclusion the objectives of standard costing are now discussed in some detail. Unless the achievement of a substantial proportion of these can be anticipated with reasonable certainty within an organisation, it is better for management concerned to reconsider the commitment of staff time to the introduction and operation of standard costing.

Standard costing systems set out to achieve synchronisation between physical stock movements and book-keeping entries. In this way it is hoped that book applications and transfers of all of the elements of cost which ultimately form the cost of sales figures in the accounts are synchronised as much as possible with the physical evidence of growth and decline of raw material, work in progress and finished goods stock levels. The linch-pin of this effort involves the creation of standard product specification sheets (SPSS) or standard cost specification sheets (SCSS), so that book entries depend at time of physical transfers upon measurement of output in units times the valuation shown on the SPSS concerned.

The achievement of budgeted levels of performance, output and costs depends upon a sufficiently high success rate at detailed product/job transaction level. Standard costs relate to specific products: if enough transactions can be generated which are in line with expectations, the result is – achievement of budgets. Standard costing relates budgets and budgetary control to detailed product levels.

Standard costing provides a vehicle for exception reporting. So long as the conversion of cash expense into stock gains is achieved on a 'pound for pound' basis, variances do not appear and reports to management advocate minimum action. As soon as the conversion process breaks down, the deviation and its cause are reported for possible remedial action.

Standard costing makes distinctions between controllable and non-controllable deviations from plan. Separation in this way ensures that management direct due time and effort to those deviations which they can counter by their own actions, while quantifying non-controllable adverse variances which require alterations to selling prices or compensating controllable favourable variances elsewhere to prevent price increases. On the same theme of ensuring optimum rather than maximum management action, standard costing distinguishes between material and trivial deviations from plan, relates compensating variances, presents cumulative variances to avoid over-reaction to seasonal fluctuations, and facilitates decisions about whether changes in operating conditions are permanent or temporary.

By requiring management to prepare detailed product specification sheets as to standard contents and their costs under normal operating conditions, standard costing should assist in the making of effective decisions on product pricing, quoting, stock valuation and profit determination, by making sure that no costs incurred in 'bringing stock to its present condition and location' are overlooked.

Detailed scrutiny of SCSS results in knowledge of appropriate cost elements, bringing possibilities for cost savings, sometimes through improved techniques. Management can frequently notice costs charged on SCSS which could be reduced or eliminated as a result of concerted action.

Clerical effort can often be greatly reduced when subsidiary records are held for individual products, processes or jobs. These need only be maintained at standard cost. Actual costs are recorded at total levels in the nominal ledger, actual and budgeted costs at departmental level (in a subsidiary ledger) but product costs can be held at standard costs. It is sometimes necessary, however, to investigate actual product costs when variances in the nominal ledger, (which show in total the deviations between actual and standard product costs), indicate that standards have deviated from actual beyond pre-defined accuracy tolerances.

Finally, standards provide a vehicle for control, motivation and improvement by setting targets related to individuals.

7 *Production Ratios*

As soon as one sets foot upon the variegated landscapes of cost accounting one is menaced by jargon: 'capacity' and 'activity' are two fine specimens unleashed by jargon at regular intervals. A clear distinction must be made between the two: the former could be described as 'hours available for possible application to production effort', and the latter, as 'the degree of application, expressed in hours'. Capacity may be a theoretical maximum, or a practical capacity.

For example, a factory could conceivably work for seven days per week, on a three shift per day basis (= 168 hours' theoretical maximum capacity). However, after discussion with employees' representatives, technical and maintenance staff, etc, it might be decided that double-shift working, for five days per week would be a more *practical* target, = (2 × 8 × 5) hours (80 hours' practical capacity). In due course, hours of actual effort might be applied directly to products for, say, 73 hours. This would be the *actual activity* achieved. If, out of a practical capacity of 80 hours, the company had planned to use 76 hours, allowing 4 hours for breakdowns, etc, they would have had a *budgeted activity* of 76 hours.

It must be noted that some companies express capacity and activity in units of saleable product rather than in hours worth of output and hours of effort. The relationship between capacity and activity remains the same, and sooner or later the companies concerned have to face up to an assessment of how many directly chargeable hours are going to be available, in determining how many units of product can be regarded as plant capacity.

The determination of capacity is important as a preliminary to preparing the *production budget*. Capacity calculation carries in its wake the useful exercise of ensuring optimum plant and manpower utilisation, to maximise the level of both theoretical maximum and practical capacities.

When theoretical maximum capacity is properly determined, a sound basis is provided for the more important practical capacity figure, which in turn is netted to provide a target *activity* level, after allowing for downtime, waiting time and other non-chargeable deductions.

Decisions can then be made about the number and size of customer orders to accept in an ensuing period, each order being converted to an hours-of-work equivalent.

When demand for a company's products is heavy, the extent to which theoretical maximum capacity has been reduced to derive practical capacity becomes critical, as does any shrinkage in hours between practical capacity and activity levels. In such situations, unbudgeted idle time/downtime necessitates improvements in efficiency ratios if budgeted output is to be achieved.

Identification of capacity levels avoids mistakes in quotations to customers regarding completion dates for work done.

The degree to which sub-contractors may be utilised can be planned in advance, to make up shortfalls between demand and capacity. Policies can be pre-planned regarding training levels, and also the degree to which re-work of damaged items can be accepted.

The possibility of acting as a sub-contractor for other companies can be discussed as a way of utilising capacity which is otherwise not required.

When capacity is analysed by department, potential bottleneck areas are identified, and corrective measures may be taken to alleviate such problems. Surplus capacity in certain departments may on occasions be used to alleviate strained resources in bottleneck areas.

Hard on the heels of certain standard costing variances come ratio counterparts.

Production Volume Ratios

As we have seen, a fixed overhead volume variance expresses the extent to which budgeted fixed overhead costs incurred have been satisfactorily converted into part of stock valuation. For example, if the budgeted fixed expenses for a period are £1,000 and targeted production is 1,000 units, a fixed overhead applied rate of £1 per unit will have been used to charge (debit) work-in-progress (cost of production), each time an actual unit of production has been achieved. In the event of 900 units being made, an unfavourable fixed overhead volume variance of £100 will cast a shadow over the company's accounts. 'The Terminology of Management and Financial Accountancy' removes the monetary implications of this situation by introducing the production volume ratio: this would tell us that the company had achieved at its actual production level, the capability to absorb 90% of budgeted fixed production overheads. The ratio is derived thus:

$$\left(\frac{\text{Actual output in units}}{\text{Budgeted output in units}} \times 100 \right)\%$$

Alternatively, the ratio is sometimes constituted as follows:

$$\left(\frac{\text{Actual activity in units}}{\text{Budgeted activity in units}} \times 100 \right)\%$$

Activity and output for this purpose are the same. In our example, we find the ratio thus:

$$\left(\frac{90}{100} \times 100 \right)\% = 90\%$$

The production volume ratio is a non-starter for variable production overheads. In our illustration, a decline in production to an actual level of 900 units would not cause any shortfall in recovery of variable overheads, as such costs would, by their very nature, decline in sympathy with and in proportion to changes in activity levels. Supposing variable costs to be budgeted at £2,000 for 1,000 units, an actual level of 900 units would create the following balance sheet situation (subject, of course, to the ravages of price/rate variances, which are another matter):

	Extract from Budgeted Balance Sheet £	Extract from Actual Balance Sheet £
Sources of Funds		
Profit and loss account	NIL	NIL
Uses of Funds		
Stock at standard cost		
(variable cost elements only)	2,000	1,800
Bank/(minus)	(2,000)	(1,800)
	NIL	NIL

When the proportion of production overheads which are fixed by nature is relatively high, a drop in production activity to below budget can be a cause for serious concern, as a manufacturing company depends in such circumstances in maintaining high activity levels. For example, when comparing two companies A and B, the following results might arise, assuming *total* standard cost per unit as £3 $\left(\frac{£3,600}{1,200} \right)$.

Company	A	B
Budgeted production	1,200 units	1,200 units
Actual production	900 units	900 units

61

Budgeted costs for 1,200 units:

Fixed (for the period)	£1,200	£ 900
Variable	£2,400	£2,700
Total	£3,600	£3,600

Actual costs for 900 units:

Fixed	£1,200	£ 900
Variable	£1,800	£2,025

The comparative balance sheets would show how the activity decline posed a greater problem for A:

	Extract from Budgeted Balance Sheet	Extract from Actual Balance Sheet
	A	B
	£	£
Sources of Funds		
Profit and loss account		
Profit/(loss)	(300)	(225)
Uses of Funds		
Stock on hand at standard (variable and fixed		
costs elements)	2,700	2,700
Bank/(minus)	(3,000)	(2,925)
	(300)	(225)

In Company A, no production has been found with which to saddle 300 × the fixed overhead recovery rate of £1. Therefore £300 has disengaged from the cost absorption mechanism, gone off to a fixed overhead volume variance account, and from there to Profit and Loss Account. In the case of Company B, the 'orphan' cost is $300 \times \frac{£900}{1200} = £225$.

Production volume ratios can be analysed into two sub-sections, provided the means are available of comparing (1) the hours which should have been taken to achieve the budgeted output, (2) the hours which should have been taken to achieve the actual output, and (3) the hours which were taken to achieve the actual output. It therefore becomes necessary to convert each budgeted unit of output to a number of hours' worth of output: if a company budgets to make 500 units of A and 1,000 units of B in a period, someone might be able to confirm that a unit of A should take 4 hours to produce, and a unit of B, 2 hours. The budgeted output would then be expressed as 4,000 standard hours. If, in due course, 400 units of A and 900 units of B were produced, this would be defined as 3,400 standard hours. The company's ability to absorb fixed costs in stock valuation would clearly be weakened by this overall result, and the production volume ratio of $\left(\frac{3,400}{4,000} \times 100\right)$% (85%) would sound the appropriate alarm bell. But if the work force, entitled to take 3,400 hours to produce the actual output, in fact completed the work in, say, 2,550 hours, what then? Firstly, the employees would clearly have worked at a high rate of efficiency. In each hour of effort, they would have achieved more than one hour's worth of output.

62

[handwritten top margin: "Prod volm" with line, "98", "Capacity booking usage"]

Their efficiency rate would have been $\left(\frac{3,400}{2,550} \times 100\right)$ % = 133% (rounded). Had they operated at the normal throughput rate, (remaining aloof, perhaps, from what was clearly something of a production crisis), the actual output would not have been 3,400 standard hours, but 2,550, the relationship between actual hours worked and standard hours allowed being one for one at 100% efficiency. So already we have derived a sub-section of the overall production volume ratio. We have a productivity (or efficiency) ratio of 133%.

The other sub-section is concerned with capacity booking and usage. Here we have a company which earmarked 4,000 hours of capacity utilisation, and no doubt deprived other managers of opportunities to use production facilities, but which used only 2,550 hours. The capacity ratio is therefore $\left(\frac{2,550}{4,000} \times 100\right)$% = 64% (rounded). This ratio, when multiplied by 133%, should give the

production volume ratio of 85% $\frac{64}{100} \times \frac{133}{100} = 85\%$ (rounded)   *[handwritten: $PV = Capacity \times Eff$]*

It is important for management to know the extent to which production facilities were actually free for an alternative use. In our example, a 64% capacity ratio would be serious indeed in the absence of a dramatic rise in the efficiency rate, *unless* some satisfactory use could be made of the balance of 1,450 hours available. The acid test would be whether the use involved production of saleable commodities which could take a share of fixed costs. The company, through its efficiency rate of 133%, has disarmed the fixed overhead absorption problem to some extent, but is still looking for other saleable production to recover 15% of total fixed expenses.

Yield and Scrap Ratios

Most standards of performance allow for a percentage of normal scrap, ie assume that a percentage of total production units will fail inspection. In such cases, good production bears the cost of itself plus a supplement to recover the cost of the scrapped units. Customers will expect such an arrangement, whereby, for example, they are charged for the cost of making 110 units when receiving 100 good units. If efficiency can be improved, they may be charged with the cost of making, say 110 units when only 5 have been scrapped. Thus, the supplier concerned has 5 extra units for sale which should have been scrapped but which are in good condition: result, increased profitability! The basic rule is that the yield percentage plus the scrap percentage = 100%. The yield percentage is basically that proportion of total output which is saleable (can carry costs to 'market').

By way of illustration: suppose that the budgeted expenses of XYZ Ltd for Period 2 were:

	£
Direct materials	50
Direct labour	100
Variable overheads	100
Fixed overheads	50
	300

[handwritten right column: "Act", "300", "60", "240", "300b"]
[handwritten middle: "300", "30 @ 10p = £3", "270", "NUC = £1.1"]

Budgeted total output was 300 units, of which 10% were expected to fail at inspection and be scrapped at a saleable value of £0·1 each. In practice, let us assume that 300 units were produced in practice, but that only 240 were saleable. The company would wish to know its yield variance and yield ratio, and its scrap ratio.

First rattle out of the box, there would be a need for a physical reconciliation of units, as follows:

	Units	Units
Total output		300

[handwritten bottom: $Yield = \frac{240}{300} = 80\%$ £33   Scrap ratio $= \frac{60}{300} = 20\%$]

Whereof:

Good units	240
Normal (expected) scrap	30
Abnormal (unexpected) scrap	30
Total accounted for	300

The yield variance would represent the amount of production cost which had become disengaged from standard good output valuation, ie the monetary amount not absorbed in 240 good units, which customers would not be expected to repay to the company via invoiced sales.

First of all, the standard valuation of one good output unit would be:

$$\frac{\text{The total cost of making 300 less any cash expected from normal scrap}}{\text{Total production less normal scrap units}}$$

$$= \frac{£(50 + 100 + 100 + 50) - £3}{300 - 30}$$

$$= \frac{£297}{£270} = £1.1 \checkmark$$

The valuation of abnormal scrap would be:

$$\text{No. of units abnormally scrapped} \times \frac{£297}{£270}$$

$$= 30 \times \frac{£297}{£270} = £33 \checkmark$$

Good output would be worth $240 \times \frac{£297}{£270} = £264$

Notice how the company, having spent a net amount of £297, have only enough good output to use as a vehicle for the recovery of £264. Had the anticipated good output of 270 units been achieved, a clean conversion of $270 \times \frac{£297}{£270}$ would have been the satisfactory outcome.

The *yield ratio* in our example is $\left(\frac{240}{300} \times 100\right)\% = 80\%$

and the *scrap ratio* is $\left(\frac{60}{300} \times 100\right)\% = 20\%$.

Should a process be involved, in which, say, a weight of output is achieved rather than a quantity of individual units, the principles remain the same. If, for example, a cook expected to derive 75% cooked meat from 4 pounds of uncooked beef, yield variance and ratio calculations could be made as follows; supposing that she charged her labour time at £2 and had overhead expenses at 40p and that actual output of cooked beef was 3·5lbs. Let us recall Halcyon days and set the price of beef as £1 per lb. Taking the physical reconciliation first:

	lbs	lbs
Total meat processed:		4
Whereby: cooked	3.5	
normal loss	1·0	
abnormal gain	(0·5)	
Total accounted for		4

On this occasion the yield variance would be favourable: half a pound of cooked beef × the normal output value per lb. This would be the value of the extra beef unexpectedly yielded from the cooking process. The value attributable to a pound of cooked beef would be:

$$\frac{£(4 + 2 + \cdot 40)}{4\text{lbs less } (25\% \times 4)} = \underline{£2 \cdot 13} \text{ (rounded)}$$

$\therefore$ The favourable yield variance would be $\underline{£1 \cdot 06}$ (rounded)

The yield ratio would be $\left(\frac{3 \cdot 5}{4} \times 100\right)\% = \underline{87 \cdot 5\%}$

The scrap ratio would be $\left(\frac{\cdot 5}{4} \times 100\right)\% = \underline{12 \cdot 5\%}$

On the dubious assumption that our cook kept accounting records, the following ledger entries would be typical:

(1)	Process Account	Dr	£6·40
	Cash	Cr	£6·40
(2)	Cooked Beef Stock	Dr	£7·46
	(3·5 × £2·13)		
	Process Account	Cr	£6·40
	Yield Variance	Cr	£1·06
(3)	Cooking Profit & Loss A/c	Dr	£7·46
	(Standard Cost of Sales)*		
	Cooked Beef Stock A/c	Cr	£7·46
(4)	Yield Variance	Dr	£1·06
	Cooking Profit & Loss A/c	Cr	£1·06

*Assuming that the cooking activity was saleable.

Supposing the cook sold the beef for £9, a price in line with standard selling prices:

Profit & Loss Account

	£
Sales at standard price	9
Standard cost of sales	7·46
Standard profit	1·54
Add: favourable yield variance	1·06
Actual profit	£2·60

	£	
Proof: Actual income	9	
actual expense	6·40	
actual profit	£2·60	

Assuming the cook's customers were willing to accept such a proposition, (and there is no apparent reason why they should not), the cook would receive as part of sales income, £1·06 to recover production costs which were not in fact incurred.

The yield variance of £1·06 above can be split into elements:

(1)	raw material yield	$\frac{1}{2}\text{lb} \times \dfrac{£4}{3\text{lbs}} = 67\text{p}$	
(2)	labour yield	$\frac{1}{2}\text{lb} \times \dfrac{£2}{3\text{lbs}} = 33\text{p}$	
(3)	overhead yield	$\frac{1}{2}\text{lb} \times \dfrac{40\text{p}}{3\text{lbs}} = 6\text{p}$	
	Total	$\underline{£1 \cdot 06}$	

If a start is made in the calculation by relating actual good output to a weight entitlement of uncooked beef, the same raw material yield variance is derived. In our example, an output of 3·5lbs involves an allowance of $(3 \cdot 5 + \frac{1}{3}rd \ of \ 3 \cdot 5) = 4 \cdot 67lbs$ of uncooked beef. (The assumption is made that 3·5lbs = raw beef input less 25%.) The actual raw beef costs was £4, and it should, according to standard, have been £1 × 4·67 = £4·67: this gives us our favourable raw beef yield of 67p.

Benefits of Ratios

In a sense, ratios serve a purpose similar to marginal costing break-even charts and profit-volume graphs: they provide easily absorbed impressions. By removing the emphasis from monetary evaluation of events, and transferring it to comparisons between actual and expected physical activities, the information conveyed often becomes clearer to non-accounting personnel. While the accounting adviser to the cook in the preceding example would calculate a favourable yield variance of £1·06, the cook in turn might prefer to focus on a yield ratio of $\left(\frac{3 \cdot 5}{4} \times 100\right) = 87 \cdot 5\%$ which provides a forthright impression of whether skills are being successfully applied. The monetary significance of a yield ratio of 87·5%, and a scrap (or wastage) ratio of $\left(\frac{\cdot 5}{4} \times 100\right) = 12 \cdot 5\%$ would make satisfying reading at a convenient moment after 'production shutdown'.

Ratios are also useful as pointers to areas which require further investigation. They put the reader on enquiry. They are particularly effective when prepared in sets to reveal trends. As with standard costing variances, each ratio should be regarded as reflecting only part of the total broad canvas of a company's affairs.

8 Marginal Costing

Standard costing probably holds first place among the techniques for cost control; but when you enter the inhospitable regions of examinations, it is helpful to remember that marginal costing can also serve as a compass in managing and reacting to expenditure. It has at its core the segregation of fixed and variable expense; costs which rise and fall in sympathy with changes in activity levels are distinguished from those which remain unaffected by such movements. Without this split, flexible budgetary control would be impossible.

Product Costs contain only Variable Elements

Marginal costing establishes an advance pattern of cost behaviour which is tested and monitored against actual results. The ensuing comparisons between actual and budgeted costs are particularly meaningful because neither budgeted nor actual fixed costs are ever re-apportioned, on some arbitrary basis, to the point of product cost comparison: this makes cost control less complicated. Product cost under marginal costing is not the *full* cost of bringing stock to its present condition and location including such items as factory rates and works manager's salary; rather it includes only costs which arise directly as a result of making each individual unit. Direct material, direct labour, and variable production overheads pass the test: fixed production overheads, for which liability to pay cash arises whether ten units are made or fifty, do not.

Cost Control Depends on Separation of Fixed and Variable Costs

A great deal of emphasis is placed on anticipating future cost levels for a range of production levels, and in discharging this function with true grit and determination, and, hopefully, professional finesse.

In short, without reliable groundwork on distinguishing between fixed and variable costs, the raison d'étre of marginal costing collapses, as its proponents know only too well. The above costs split also happens to be the foundation for comparing actual with budgeted costs, which is the centre point of cost control.

An Aid to Product Selection

If many production costs arise simply because there is a production function which is operational, it is good business to make and sell products which generate as little variable cost as possible, in their own right, so that a high proportion of sales income is left over after those variable product costs have been paid. Each product sold, should, hopefully, make as high a *contribution* to communal fixed costs as possible. So, if a product costs £50 in direct materials, direct labour and variable overhead, the principles are clear:

(1) should the product not be made, bills for £50 ought not to be received by the manufacturer;

(2) should the product be made and sold for more than £50, it will generate a contribution to the other costs which will undoubtedly be faced simply because there is a factory in operation;

(3) should these other costs be high, the company has to generate enough small contributions from a large quantity of sales to clear them, or enough large contributions from a smaller quantity;

(4) 'profit per unit' loses its significance, and is replaced by 'contribution per unit'.

Contribution per unit is the difference between the selling price of a unit and its variable, or marginal cost. The variable cost of a unit is that cost which would be avoided if the unit was not produced or provided.

Operating Results from Marginal Costing Techniques

Irresistible tides now draw us swiftly forward. From its total sales, variable costs and fixed costs a company can learn about its operational health. To illustrate, assume that Company A has:

Sales	£60,000
Variable expenses	£36,000
Fixed expenses	£6,000

Firstly, the *contribution margin ratio* can be calculated. Out of sales income of £60,000, the company must set aside £36,000 to pay for direct material, direct labour and variable overheads. This leaves £24,000 clear as profit . . . but wait! Before too much rejoicing is condoned, we must remember the £6,000 which must also be paid. The £24,000 contributes, then, towards fixed expenses and profit. The contribution ratio is $\left(\frac{24,000}{60,000} \times 100\right)\% = 40\%$. The pattern has emerged that out of each £1 of sales, 60p has to be set aside to pay for inevitable variable costs, and 40p is available to be either pocketed as profit or paid out to help clear fixed costs.

Secondly, *break-even sales* should be derived. From each £1 of sales, 40p is generated to help the company break-even. The break-even point is reached when enough 40p's are achieved to surmount the problem of total fixed costs with nothing to spare. At this point, the company is making neither a profit nor a loss. In our example, each £1 of sales achieved takes us one step to-wards our objective to the tune of 40p. Therefore we need to take quite a number of steps to reach £6,000! Exactly how many? $\frac{£6,000}{40p} = 15,000$. That is, when sales reach £15,000, company costs will be $15,000 \times 60p$ (variable) $= £9,000$, plus £6,000 (fixed) $= £15,000$, and profit will be NIL. At break-even point, sales less variable expenses = fixed costs plus a nil profit. Representing this in digit format, $S - V = F + P$ (0). Any sales made beyond break-even point generate a con-tribution, as before, but each 40p per £1 of additional sales need not be expended in trying to soak up part of the £6,000 fixed costs: each 40p will be a contribution only to profits.

If the number of product units is known, the break-even point can be expressed as the number of units at which the company makes neither a profit nor a loss. If £60,000 of sales in our example represents 1,000 units, the break-even point of £15,000 of sales can be expressed as 250 units $\left(\frac{15,000}{60,000} \times 1,000\right)$.

The *variable cost ratio* emanates naturally from calculating the contribution ratio: it is that part of sales income which must be set aside to pay the variable costs related to those sales, expressed as a percentage. In our example the ratio is: $\left(\frac{36,000}{60,000} \times 100\right)\% = 60\%$. As you can see, the variable cost and the contribution ratios = 100%. The higher the variable cost ratio for a particular product, the less enthusiasm can be raised for taking the trouble to make it.

The *amount* of the *margin of safety* can also be calculated. This shows the extent to which sales can take a tumble from their present level before reaching the fateful break-even point. Once sales have slumped below break-even point, the company is failing to generate enough 40p's to clear total fixed expenses, and is therefore making a loss. In our illustration, present sales of £60,000 are £45,000 above break-even point of £15,000. The margin of safety is £45,000 (or 750 units).

The *percentage margin of safety* shows the percentage decline in present sales which can be tolerated before the company reaches break-even point: $\left(\frac{45,000}{60,000} \times 100\right)\% = 75\%$.

Interpretation of Results

Each of the above items of information is highly significant to management. In times of inflation, for example, a product for which the selling price is pegged by legislation or market pressure can lose much of its appeal if it has a high variable cost ratio and is vulnerable to escalating variable costs. Such products have a nasty habit of burning up valuable production capacity which could have been used to greater effect. The costs of having capacity available and in maintained, serviceable condition tend to be 'fixed expense', as does plant depreciation involved, and management have an unending struggle to ensure as low a variable cost ratio as possible, especially when capacity is not fully utilised. When a company is determined to finance future growth out of its own operations, any success in this field depends on maintaining a tight grip on variable cost ratios, or, conversely, increasing contribution ratios. In times when all customer orders are gratefully received, because capacity usage is depressed, pressure to cut back on the variable cost ratio is relentless; as unit contribution ratios are in short supply, they have to be as large as possible.

The relationship of total fixed cost to total variable cost is very important. For example, a variable cost ratio of 90%, if at first sight alarming, could be highly satisfactory if a company had a budget to produce and sell 200,000 units, each selling at £1, and if the fixed expense budget was, say, £4,000. The capture of 10p as a contribution for each £1 of sales would provide £20,000 to clear £4,000, with a resultant profit of £16,000. Individual ratios should not be used in isolation.

The percentage margin of safety is vital in a dubious market, where customer demand is volatile, or, in the case of a new product, not tested by direct experience. Simulation can take place, in that budgeted sales can be substituted for present sales in calculating the extent to which budgeted sales can be 'misjudged' before disaster strikes.

Armed with the sales, variable expense and fixed expense totals above, the effects of possible deviations can be measured. For example, influenced possibly by the amount of capital employed in the venture, our company A might wish to know the sales level required to achieve a profit of £10,000. In such cases, replace profit required with contribution required, and calculate the number of individual contribution steps per £1 of sales which need to be taken to overtake the total required contribution. Thus, company A needs a contribution of £16,000 to ensure its profit of £10,000. Forty pence is achieved towards this goal with each £1 of sales. Therefore the required sales level is $\dfrac{£16,000}{40p} = £40,000$.

Again, suppose that fixed expenses can be reduced by £2,000, but a sales price reduction of 10% is needed. What is the new break-even point? Total sales income will decline by 10% to £54,000 with variable costs remaining at £36,000. (We cannot expect a cost reduction just because we are discounting the selling price!). From each £1 of sales a contribution of $\left(\dfrac{18,000}{54,000} \times 100\right)$p will be achieved (33p). Therefore the new break-even point is:

$$\frac{£4,000 \text{ fixed costs}}{33p} = £12,000$$

Alternatively, in the event of variable costs rising by 10%, and reverting otherwise to the original figures the new break-even point would be:

$$\frac{£6,000}{34p} = £17,648 \text{ (rounded)}$$

$$(\text{Contribution ratio} = \left(\frac{£(60,000-39,600) = £20,400}{60,000} \times 100\right)\% = 34\%)$$

Unrestricted Facilities and Resources

When there is an unlimited supply of the resources needed to produce units for sale, competition among individual product types or categories for a share of these resources, including production capacity, lies dormant.

In such cases, all customer orders should be welcomed provided they afford a contribution to the company's fixed expenses. The name of the game is to try somehow to improve the mix of customer orders, so that products with high contributions make up an ever increasing proportion of total sales.

The Risks in Absorption Costing

When marginal costing is dispensed with, attempts are made to spread fixed expenses on an equitable basis across a company's product range. The results obtained often show a degree of precision and credibility which is unjustified, as arbitrary guesswork can be at the root of the problem of dealing with fixed costs, and can have a significant bearing on which product is the most 'profitable'. Fixed costs can be apportioned (or spread) by a number of different methods, and if two accountants, working independently, were to tackle a particular exercise in this field, they might well produce significantly different results. Let us examine the results of one such fixed costs apportionment exercise, undertaken for a company manufacturing and selling three products, X, Y and Z. Imaginary figures are used.

	Product X	Product Y	Product Z
Annual production	1,000 units	1,000 units	1,000 units
	£	£	£
Selling price per unit	35	66	55
Total costs:			
Variable	15,000	39,000	32,000
Fixed	11,000	28,000	19,000
	26,000	67,000	51,000
Cost per unit	26	67	51
Profit/(loss) per unit	9	(1)	4
Profit/(loss) on 1,000 units	9,000	(1,000)	4,000
		£12,000	

The above figures pertaining to product Y would make a distinctly disagreeable impression upon management, who would fasten hopefully upon the effects of removing this ailing product from the scene.

The removal of Product Y could, however, be disastrous, as it is presently absorbing and recovering £28,000 of fixed expense, a task which would fall upon the two surviving products in the event of Y's demise, unless the fixed expense vanished along with Y. Much of the £28,000 would be general establishment cost such as factory rates and works managers' salaries which would go on apace after reduction of the product range. Other parts of this sum would relate directly to product Y, such as foremen's salaries and depreciation of machinery specifically deployed on production of Y.

A simplified marginal costing statement would warn against over-zealous use of the axe.

	With Product Y £	Without Product Y £
Sales	156,000	90,000
Variable costs	86,000	47,000
Contribution	70,000	43,000
Total fixed costs*	58,000	58,000
Total profit/(loss)	12,000	(15,000)

*assuming all fixed costs would remain after Y's elimination. Depreciation on machinery used solely in producing Y would not be avoided by removing Y, merely accelerated as a charge. There would be an immediate write-off of any balance of value remaining in the books for that machinery, rather than a phased write-off through annual depreciation charges. The dramatic decision as to whether to reduce the product range would depend on longer term plans for the additional capacity suddenly available. The real issue would not be as clear-cut as implied above. There could, for example, be the prospect of making a fourth product in due course, with which some of the dreaded fixed costs of this struggling organisation could become associated. Again, the newly idle capacity could be sub-contracted; or it could have a separate physical identity whereby a wing of the factory could, in fact, be closed down with a genuine substantial saving in total fixed costs.

In the example above, the respective contribution ratios of X, Y and Z are:

$$X: \left(\frac{35,000-15,000}{35,000} \times 100 \right)\% = 71\% \text{ (rounded)}$$

$$Y: \left(\frac{66,000-39,000}{66,000} \times 100 \right)\% = 41\% \text{ (rounded)}$$

$$Z: \left(\frac{55,000-32,000}{55,000} \times 100 \right)\% = 41\% \text{ (rounded)}$$

While X is head and shoulders above Y and Z in terms of contribution generated per £1 of sales, Y has as much to commend it as Z when sales campaigns are planned in the future.

Visual Charts

Visual presentation comes into its own when marginal costing is used. With the distinctions between fixed and variable costs established and the nettle of their separation firmly grasped, management can simulate likely cost behaviour at various activity levels.

Basically, the *break-even* and the *profit/volume (P/V)* graphs are helpful to non-accounting personnel to provide quick general impressions on potential profits, at varying activity levels. Confucius he say: 'One picture is worth a thousand words'.

Break-even Graphs

The break-even graph (or chart) has a monetary value perpendicular axis, with activity levels, either in units or monetary value equivalents, being depicted on the horizontal axis. The latter axis shows, therefore, a wide range of possible activity options which may or may not become targets for future operations. In times of straitened circumstances, the graph may be prepared defensively to show how far a company might safely retreat in terms of market share before serious harm was inflicted, or how damaging particular sales discounting policies or cost inflation might be. A break-even graph is a simulation model which depicts the relationship of costs to

71

sales turnover over a wide range of activity levels. The effects of changing one or more of the cost or income constituents can be displayed by re-positioning whichever of the (1) sales, (2) variable cost, (3) fixed cost lines are affected. Actual firm plans are frequently represented by unbroken lines with possible amendments projected through broken or dotted lines.

The ensuing break-even graph, which illustrates the relationships of costs to sales, has been prepared from the following information:

Company A manufactures and sells product X. The selling price per unit is £20, and variable costs per unit are £8. Fixed expenses related to product X are £20,000. The budged turnover for the ensuing accounting period is £120,000. Management are concerned that the planned selling price of £20 may not be achieved in practice, and wish to measure the effects on profits of a 5% discount. At the same time, the fixed costs may prove difficult to peg at £20,000, and a further £5,000 'safety margin' is now required.

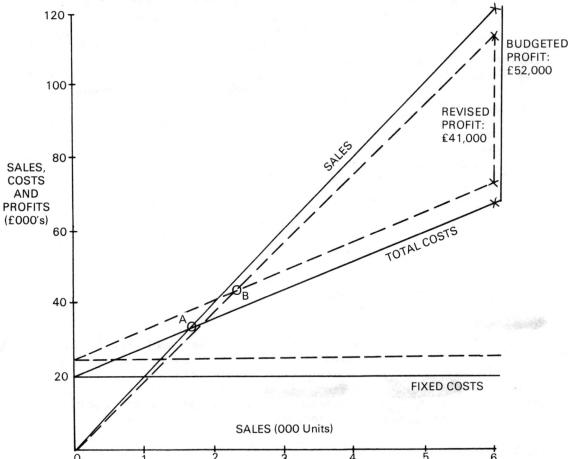

The break-even point A shows the more optimistic (budgeted) situation, with the selling price at £20 per unit, and with variable and fixed costs at £8 per unit and £20,000 for the period. The further the break-even point can be pushed to the left, the better. Revised forecasts of selling price and fixed costs have, however, driven the break-even point further along the activity scale to the right at (B), although the situation is still refreshingly healthy.

A and B can be calculated as follows:

	A	B
Contribution per unit	£(20–8) = £12	£(19–8) = £11
Break-even point	$\dfrac{£20,000}{12} = 1,667$ units	$\dfrac{£25,000}{11} = 2,273$ units

(1) The budgeted profit and (2) the revised profit are:

(1) £120,000–£((6,000 × 8) + 20,000) = <u>£52,000</u>

(2) £114,000–£((6,000 × 8) + 25,000) = <u>£41,000</u>

Some break-even graph presentations project sales and variable costs from the zero-point at which the perpendicular and horizontal axis join. In such cases, the break-even points are identical to those previously depicted and calculated.

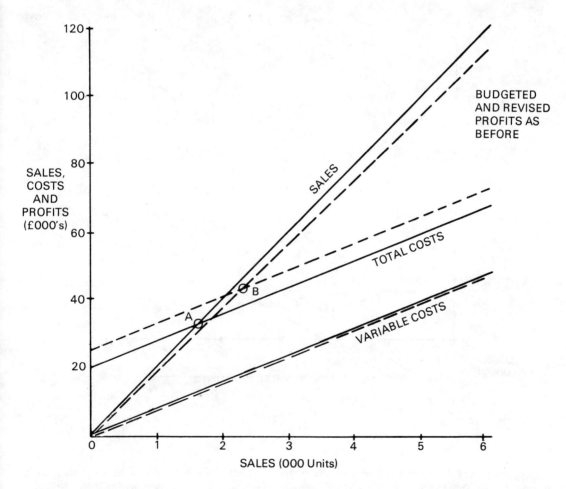

If preferred, break-even point may be expressed as the sales turnover figure at which the company achieves neither a profit nor a loss:

A: 1,667 units × £20 = <u>£33,340</u>

B: 2,273 units × £19 = <u>£43,187</u>

Proof: A: $S - V = F + P$

∴ £(33,320–13,336) = £20,000 + NIL
(The difference of £16 is due to rounding.)
B: £43,187–18,184 = £25,000 + NIL
(The difference of £3 is due to rounding.)

Profit/Volume Graphs

The function of visually presenting the above information can be discharged with equal success using a *profit/volume graph*. A single, horizontal line representing volumes of activity abuts on the perpendicular axis at right angles. Across the activity line, a contribution line sweeps from a starting point at which the company, at zero activity, makes a loss exactly equal to the total fixed expenses:

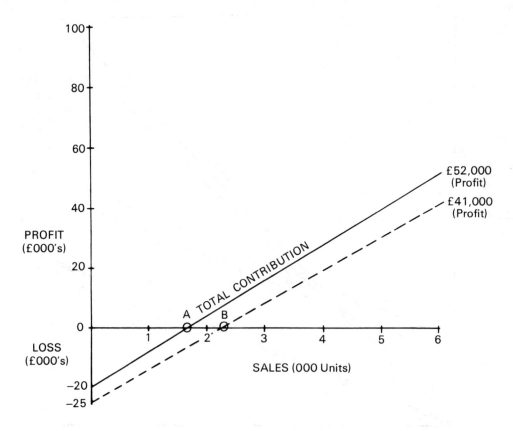

Management examine the sharpness of the degree of climb of the total contribution line, as it moves away from the loss-making start point at the base of the perpendicular axis. As each budgeted unit of sale is achieved, ie as the total unbroken contribution line edges one unit to the right on the horizontal axis, £12 of the total loss of £20,000 is eliminated; similarly, using the provisional adjusted figures, the dotted line moves up the perpendicular scale by £11 for each movement it makes of one unit to the right. The total contribution using the selling price of £20 is £(20–8) × 6,000 units = £72,000, but of this amount, £20,000 has to be set aside to pay off fixed expenses, leaving a profit of £52,000 as shown. Using £19 as the selling price, the total contribution is £(19–8) × 6,000 = £66,000, but £25,000 of projected fixed costs cuts the profit to £41,000.

Uses of Break-even and Profit/Volume Graphs

Having invested break-even and profit-volume graphs with some sort of illustrative practical background, we can examine the main uses of these visual aids to management in more detail. They:

(1) illustrate the inter-acting effects on profits, cost and revenue levels of making decisions to change selling prices, sales volumes, unit variable costs or fixed costs.
(2) illustrate the degree of safety-margin between a company's actual activity level and that activity level at which it will make neither a profit nor a loss, and show the change in that safety margin which would be brought about by the decisions at (1) above.
(3) show, all else being equal, the effect of physical volume changes on the profits of the company. (Some managers consider that while a BREAK-EVEN CHART shows such effects, the PROFIT/VOLUME CHART (GRAPH) *highlights* these effects.)
(4) force management to project future costs with reasonable accuracy, ie costs projected on the basis of a budget for an anticipated activity level, or range of levels, and to face up to the challenge of recognising cost behavioural patterns, especially the basic distinction between fixed and variable costs.
(5) illustrate the importance of increased turnover, emphasising particularly in the case of profit-volume graphs the value of an additional contribution margin for each unit of activity after break-even point.
(6) assist in the education of non-accounting staff.
(7) provide explanatory charts for sales staff watching trends from year to year.
(8) show how soon new plants can be made profitable.

Comparisons Within a Mix of Products

In addition, profit-volume charts are particularly useful for making comparisons of performance within a mix of products. The angle of climb for each product can be shown, indicating the extent to which each product makes a contribution towards the recovery of fixed expenses and profit from each £1 of sales achieved. The sharper the angle of climb, the more pence can be utilised out of £1 of sales towards contribution. This technique is effective in choosing which products to eliminate from a range, in order to enrich the product mix, so that higher contributions can be generated from the same total level of sales, (the sales lost when certain products are eliminated being made up by remaining products to the original total).

For example, if, say, four products were involved and required inclusion on a profit-volume graph, information regarding sales values and variable costs could lead to the calculations shown below in the right-hand columns 5, 6(a) and 6(b):

1	2	3	4	5	6	
	Sales	Variable	Fixed	Profit/	Calculated	
Product	Value	Costs	Costs	(Loss)	contributions	
					(a)	(b)
	£	£	£	£	£	%
A	30,000	21,000	8,000	1,000	9,000	30
B	40,000	36,000	2,000	2,000	4,000	10
C	50,000	32,000	4,000	14,000	18,000	36
D	60,000	51,000	11,000	(2,000)	9,000	15
	180,000	140,000	25,000	15,000		

The information could then be depicted on a profit-volume graph as follows:

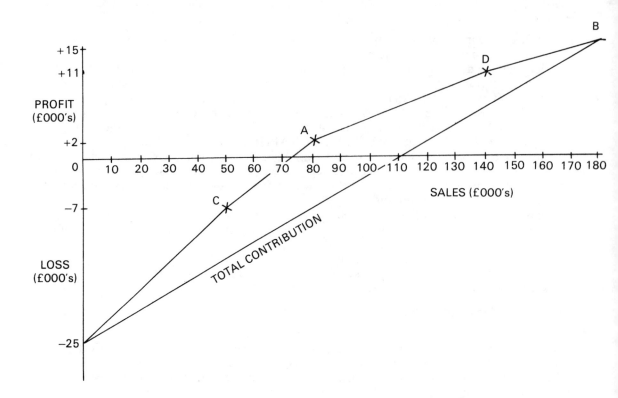

This profit-volume graph shows the usual total contribution line, between a start point of a £25,000 loss on the perpendicular axis at zero sales activity, and, at the top right hand side, a point at which sales have reached £180,000 on the horizontal axis and a profit of £15,000 has been achieved on the perpendicular axis. The products have been 'sent in to bat' in descending order of performance, ie the best contributor towards fixed expenses and profit per £ of sales is C, and the effect of C's total sales on eating up a large portion of the fixed expenses total of £25,000 has been shown first. Notice how the angle of climb of the C–A–D–B line has flattened out towards the top right hand end. B is the product which offers the poorest contribution of the four (10%).

Clearly, the profit of the organisation in the preceding example could be enhanced by restricting the number of products, provided that the lost sales could be spread across the remaining products. If the least attractive product B were eliminated, and its sales spread across A, C and D in proportion to their present sales levels of £30,000, £50,000 and £60,000 respectively, the situation would be as follows:

Product	Sales Value (see calculation)	Variable costs	Calculated contributions (a)	(b)
	£	£	£	%
A	38,571	27,000	11,571	30
C	64,286	41,143	23,143	36
D	77,143	65,571	11,572	15
	180,000	133,714	46,286	
		Less fixed expenses	25,000	
		Revised profit	£21,286	

Calculation of revised sales values

Product	Present turnover	Proportional increase		Revised Sales
	£		£	£
A	30,000	$\frac{3}{14} \times £40,000$	8,571	38,571
C	50,000	$\frac{5}{14} \times £40,000$	14,286	64,286
D	60,000	$\frac{6}{14} \times £40,000$	17,143	77,143
	£140,000		£40,000	£180,000

A comparison of the original four-product situation with that arising from eliminating product B and spreading its sales as above, can be made on our original profit-volume graph, overleaf.

Notice how the horizontal line still only extends to £180,000, but the new dotted lines, terminating at D_2, recover £25,000 of fixed expenses plus £21,286 towards profit. The figures of (1) $-1 \cdot 857$, (2) $+9 \cdot 714$ and (3) $+21 \cdot 286$ on the perpendicular axis are the loss (–) and profit (+) figures after achieving sales of (1) C only (at the new level), (2) C + A (at the new levels), and (3) C + A + D at the new levels. Clearly, this exercise could be repeated without D which is now the poorest product, but one has to remember that there are many sound commercial reasons for maintaining a wide product range, especially in a fickle market. In fact, management in the preceding example would think long and hard before activitating the dotted lines which would herald the demise of product B.

Difficulties of Utilising Marginal Costing

The following aspects can render marginal costing a troublesome technique to employ.

(1) *Classification of costs:* the distinction between fixed and variable cost elements may be difficult to determine for such items as idle time costs, overtime premiums, and maintenance and repairs. The use of break-even charts and profit volume graphs which use straight-line curves tends to depend on clear-cut distinctions between fixed and variable costs.

(2) *Use of projections:* marginal costing is often used to try to anticipate the future. It is useful in ideal conditions as a forward planning technique, but its use depends on a full range of projections any one or more of which could be materially erroneous. For example, an assumption is necessary that the market will happily respond to increased availability of a

77

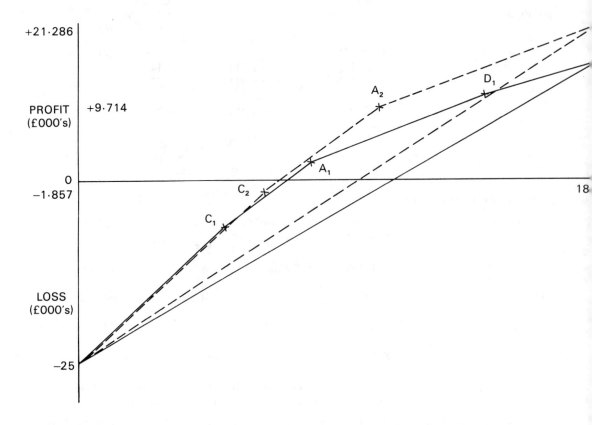

product should the company expand its capacity usage. Assumptions need to be made regarding the prices at which future sales may be achieved, and so on.

(3) *Assumptions re Sales and Production:* straight-line graphs depicting changes in profits from changes in activity levels assume that whatever is made can be sold, and whatever is to be sold can be produced. Sometimes forward projections of production capacity limits are not known until actually put to the test.

(4) *Influencing factors:* beyond certain activity (ie capacity usage) scales, new factors can exert an influence both on costs and on quality. Changes in plant scale and/or technology become necessary and their influence can only be surmised until actual experience crystalises the facts.

(5) *One set of assumptions depicted:* visual presentations as well as figure-work reports present true and fair pictures using one set of assumptions. If one of these assumptions should prove faulty, the whole canvas has to be re-drawn.

(6) *One mix of products assumed:* the use of straight-line curves on break-even and profit-volume graphs again assumes a constant mix of products, ie that the proportion of sales of each product to the total sales of all products is constant at all levels of activity. This may or may not be a misleading assumption depending on the nature of the business involved and its market characteristics.

(7) *Stock valuation at variable cost:* the contribution to fixed costs and profit earned by each product is calculated under marginal costing. This involves valuation of stock at variable

cost only; consequently, stock requires to be revalued to comply with audit and annual accounts specifications.

(8) *Aid to pricing policy may be reduced*: there is a school of thought which advocates the attachment of full cost to each product to ensure that there is no oversight in determining necessary prices to recover all overheads. Proponents of full (or absorption) costing emphasise that the absorption of full cost by each product ensures that selling and marketing functions are left in no doubt as to their task in ensuring successful sales campaigns which effectively provide the only means of recovering a wide range of costs some of which may not be readily apparent.

(9) *Usefulness depends on capacity usage*: marginal costing techniques are often extended to determine which products should be made when one or more production resource is scarce (or limited). In such circumstances, the market is not the limiting factor which acts as the restraint on continuing growth. However, many companies now find that they have more capacity than they need to fulfil customer orders, and in such cases the exploitation of the more interesting and rewarding aspects of marginal costing is curtailed.

(10) *Changing circumstances:* as time passes, many organisations are finding that a lower proportion of total costs can be regarded as variable by nature. In addition, the 'variable' costs which remain are becoming more and more unreliable as regards their behaviour in the face of activity changes. The higher the proportion of total costs which are insensitive to activity changes, the less useful marginal costing may become, but, again, this may depend on circumstances, in that a very low percentage of variable cost may be critical when profit margins are very 'tight'.

BEST USE OF LIMITED RESOURCES

When man-hours, or machine hours or some other resources are in short supply, it becomes necessary for a company to determine the products from their range which offer the greatest contribution, not per unit, but per unit of limiting factor. In this way each unit of scarce resource is put to the most profitable use. The company wishes in such cases to generate the highest fixed overhead recovery rate per hour over a limited number of hours, or, perhaps the highest rate per £1 of raw materials, if such be the 'limiting factor'. Typical limiting (or 'key' factors) which can restrict a company's activity are: (a) machine-hours, (b) man-hours and (c) raw material resources, either expressed in terms of a raw material monetary value, or as a quantity. Thus, when market demand exceeds a company's ability to produce, the company should try to be selective in the way that it exhausts whatever production resource is scarce. For example, three products could produce the following contributions per unit:

Product	A	B	C
	£	£	£
Sales value per unit	10	8	7
Variable costs per unit	6	3	5
Contribution per unit	4	5	2

Supposing man-hours to be the limiting factor, the usage rate in man-hours per product unit might be as follows:

Product	A	B	C
Man-hours per unit	3	3	1

79

Each time one man-hour is burned up, it should earn the highest available contribution. Production capacity should be booked on this basis, so that the market demand for the product with the highest contribution per man-hour is fully satisfied first: because of shortage of production facilities, the market demand of the poorer contributor product(s) will, of course, never be satisfied.

In the preceding example, therefore, product B is toppled from its perch and product C (surprisingly) gains the ascendancy, the contributions per unit of limiting factor being:

$$A, £\frac{4}{3} = £1 \cdot 33, B, £\frac{5}{3} = £1 \cdot 66, C, £\frac{2}{1} = £2.$$

In the event of man-hours being restricted to 1,000 for the accounting period concerned, and market demand for A, B and C being 250 in each case, the maximum contribution which could be earned would be:

Products in order of priority	No. of units	Hrs per unit	Plant utilisation (hours)	Total contribution £
C	250	1	250	500
B	250	3	750	1,250
A	—	–	—	—
	500		1,000	£1,750

This branch of the technique of marginal costing would suggest the abandonment of the company's interest in product A: provided that the limit on man-hours remained at 1,000. In practice, other factors would need to be weighed such as relative market security of each product.

Failure to recognise the significance of man-hours as the limiting factor would attract management towards the following 'maximum' contributions:

Products in order of priority	No. of units	Plant utilisation (hours)	Total contribution £
B	250	750	1,250
A	83	250	332
C	–	—	—
		1,000	£1,582

Irresistible tides could draw management towards withdrawing production facilities from product C, which is in fact the product to be preferred in the given circumstances.

The following example will illustrate more of the principles involved: Beta Limited manufactures three components, X, Y & Z, which it sells throughout the electrical industry and which are made up from three parts, Zeta, Eeta and Theta in the following proportions:

Component	Parts
X	1 Zeta and 1 Eeta
Y	2 of Zeta, 2 of Eeta and 1 of Theta
Z	3 of Zeta, 1 of Eeta and 2 of Theta

The parts mentioned above are made on the premises. Further information is as follows:

	Zeta	Eeta	Theta
Selling prices	£6	£14	£24
Direct materials	£2	£2	£5
Time cost	£2	£9	£12

'Time cost', which covers the cost of direct labour and overheads, is valued at £6 per hour. All parts can be sold individually at the above selling prices, but the market demand which it is hoped will be satisfied from the expansion will be for the components. The further expansion would provide an additional 5,800 hours. Additional market demand for the components is as follows:

X: 5,000 units
Y: 5,000 units
Z: 5,000 units

Additional fixed expenses related to the expansion are expected to be £15,000.

Required: prepare a statement showing how the additional capacity available should be used to generate maximum additional profit.

Solution

	X	Y	Z
Sales price per unit	20	64	80
Variable costs: material	4	13	18
conversion	11	34	39
	15	47	57
Contribution per unit (£)	5	17	23
Hours required per unit	$1\frac{5}{6}$	$5\frac{2}{3}$	$6\frac{1}{2}$
Contribution per hour	£2·7	£3	£3·5 (rounded)
Rating of products for:			
Usage of capacity	3rd	2nd	1st
Market demand (units)	5,000	5,000	5,000
Production requirements (hrs)	9,167	28,334	32,500

Production scheduling:	UNITS	Hours Used	Contribution
Z	5,000	32,500	113,750
Y	4,500	25,500	76,500
Total hours available		58,000	190,250
Fixed overheads			15,000
Highest profit			£175,250

Again, several factories within a group could be competing for orders: each factory might offer a different mix of resources, say man-hours and machine hours, and the problem would involve selection of the most economic order placement across available factories, so that resources were used to best advantage.

Relevant and Irrelevant Costs

Marginal costing is used to determine the best course of action from a number of business options: in such cases costs tend to be split into those which are fixed or constant for all possible options, and variable according to which option is being evaluated. Costs which are constant to all options are classed as 'irrelevant', because they do not influence the choice of option. Consider the following question: In a factory, direct materials costs £3 per production unit. A proposal has been made to re-arrange plant facilities, and thus improve efficiency by increasing throughput of units. It is considered that while 8 units are passed through in one hour under present arrangements, efficiency in this respect could be raised to 125% if the plant layout were re-organised. Direct labour costs £4 per hour. Management want to know whether it makes economic sense to authorise the plant re-organisation.

In this case, the first task of whoever is preparing the accounting report which will influence management is to define the company's options. These are: (1) re-arrange facilities, (2) do not re-arrange facilities. Then must come the identification of costs which are common or constant for both options. Direct materials are in this category: whichever way the cat jumps, the company will pay £3 per unit. Then, the reporter must decide whether there is any merit in including 'irrelevant' costs on his report layout. From time to time he might think that the effects of options on profits would be highly significant to his readers: the penalty for this choice is of course the inclusion of all costs as a cost of sales total against sales income, whether or not the former vary with alternative courses of action. In our example, there is no question of any attempt being made to relate the company's options to an overall profit statement. Consequently, the report should be a very small affair:

	PER UNIT	
	(1)	(2)
Option	Re-arrange	Do not re-arrange
	£	£
Direct labour	40p	50p
Differential in favour of (1)		10p

The decision should be taken to re-arrange.

The direct labour charges of (1) 40p and (2) 50p per unit are arrived at as follows:

(1) $\frac{125}{120} \times 8 \text{ units} = 10$ $\therefore$ Unit rate $= \dfrac{£4 \text{ per hour}}{10 \text{ units per hour}} = 40\text{p}$

(2) $\dfrac{£4 \text{ per hour}}{8 \text{ units per hour}} = 50\text{p}$

Broader issues will always be involved than are apparent from the slender indications of direct cost comparison, and management would be unlikely to draw final conclusions on a course of action without considering whether changes would have an unsettling effect upon the workforce, customers, or other areas of production. Overheads, not mentioned in our simplified example, would probably be affected and would thus constitute 'relevant' costs. Faster throughput in one area of production could certainly mean bottlenecks elsewhere.

The segregation of relevant from irrelevant costs is the linchpin of choosing the best course of action from a range of options. For example, a choice might be necessary between accepting a customer's special order at an abnormal rate or rejecting it; or the possibility of sub-contracting production (or not) might need assessment. There is a tendency for fixed costs to be the centre point of irrelevant costs, but there is no basis in such a comment for a golden rule. Moreover, it is sometimes prudent to show irrelevant fixed costs (common to all options) on statements to warn readers that perhaps a subjective view has been taken that fixed costs will in no way vary from option to option, and that this view is based on assumptions which should be probed.

Again, readers must be allowed to ask whether an assumption that variable costs per unit will be identical for a particular element such as materials at two or more activity levels is soundly based. Accountants tend to assume, for the purposes of simplicity and clarity of presentation, that total variable costs of production rise and fall in direct proportion to levels of production activity, ie the variable unit cost rate is constant. This assumption can be faulty primarily because projected or forecast costs are involved for levels of activity at which the company concerned may have had little or no experience.

UNIT RATES CAN BE DISTORTED

Variable costs rise and fall for reasons other than changes in unit volumes. Pressures of supply of and demand for the various resources which are needed for operations cause distortions to 'standardised' unit rates. For example:

(a) after a certain activity level has been reached, an extra shift may be necessary which requires additional payments to direct operatives, automatically raising unit costs.

(b) supplies of optimum grades of labour or raw materials may cease after a certain production level has been reached. As a result, changes emerge to scrap levels, production times and re-work schedules for faulty items. Conversely, bulk discounts on raw materials may become payable after certain levels of purchases, lowering the unit raw material price.

(c) changes in techniques may be needed at certain levels of production eg involving less than ideal machinery and/or higher scrap levels: conversely, economies of scale may only become possible at certain minimum output levels.

(d) below certain levels of activity certain variable costs may become fixed: for example, a minimum direct labour work-force costing far in excess of standard may be essential to provide a basis for resurgence.

(e) output levels per departmental, machine or direct labour hour may not be consistent owing to changes in tiredness and concentration levels, motivation levels, etc.

9 Concurrent Use of Marginal and Standard Costing

It is a common belief in industry that a company ought to strive at all times to increase its sales turnover, and, if at all possible, its market share. The view is held that increases in a company's turnover do not result in proportionate increases in cost levels. Moreover, the higher the proportion of total cost per unit which is fixed, (ie which represents a share of those operating costs which are incurred because facilities merely exist, and which are insensitive to the level of usage of those facilities), the more satisfactory is each increase by one unit of sale beyond the company's break-even point. For example, if a company's selling price per unit of product is £10, it will need to manufacture and sell 4,000 units to break-even, if its variable costs per unit are £7 and the fixed costs to be absorbed total £12,000. (Each unit sold provides a contribution of £3, £(10–7), towards absorbing £12,000 of fixed cost. Therefore 4,000 units are needed to absorb £12,000 at the rate of £3 per unit.) As soon as the 4,000 units mark is overtaken, £3 per unit is achieved towards profit.

In fact, if a company's actual production activity can climb above budgeted production activity, a fixed production overhead volume variance will measure the extent to which the company can attempt, if it so wishes, to recover fixed costs from customers which have not in fact been incurred, provided budgeted and actual fixed expenses are the same. Later, at the point of sale, a further volume variance, the sales volume variance, emerges if sales activity exceeds or falls short of budgeted sales activity. Each of the variances described above is a profit variance and each is very important to an industrial concern. Even those who have no partiality for, or who question the aptness of marginal costing, sense that high turnover means clearance of the hurdle of fixed costs, and that low turnover can spell disaster.

If an increased turnover against budget can be linked to an increase in market share, the principle is that competitors' turnovers should be in decline, leaving them less capable of absorbing their fixed expenses in sales, (unless they make themselves less competitive by increasing their prices). Increasing market share draws the company concerned into prominence, if not predominance. Possibilities loom large for more aggressive marketing policies, and for playing a greater role in competitive pricing strategy. Both favourable volume variances and greater market share can aid flexibility in pricing, and distinct possibilities emerge for discounting and for 'special offer' pricing.

Sales Turnover Increases must be Looked at with Care

Increases in sales turnover may conceal problems:

(a) Monetary turnover increases must be related to quantity increases. It is quite possible to add 50% to monetary turnover while doubling quantity turnover, with potentially disastrous results, as the total cost of sales figure in such circumstances will be a sorry spectacle.

(b) While turnover increases may well denote popularity of products on the market, it may also indicate that goods are underpriced. When under-pricing is acute long-term damage can readily result, eg from failure to recover fixed overheads and from bad publicity when prices are finally raised.

(c)   While total monetary turnover may increase, product sales mix within total bulk may deviate from standard mix, with sales of products with poor unit contributions to fixed expenses and profits exceeding expectations, and high contributor products faring badly. In simple terms, this could mean that an increase in total costs could more than offset any increase in monetary turnover.

(d)   Increased turnover, whether or not substantial volume variances result, may be achieved at the expense of incurring unfavourable cost variances, particularly for selling expenses. Increased turnover may also have strained production capacity, with resulting adverse production variances caused by hurried training, re-deployment of non-standard grades of labour, and use of non-standard grades of material purchased from unfamiliar resources.

(e)   Unbudgeted increases in sales quantity turnover can erode closing stock quantities so that the marketing plans for the ensuing period are damaged.

(f)   An uncritical acceptance of work-loads results in the commitment of valuable production capacity which thus becomes unavailable should more profitable work be offered at a later date.

opportunity cost

(g)   When increased market share is a potential prize, business has to be wrested from competitors. Management may be puzzled to find their true course and duty; should they facilitate matters by improving quality at the expense of escallating costs?

(h)   Putting competitors out of business will naturally put a greater burden on surviving companies to produce more, and this may be sound in theory, but prove impossible in practice. In such circumstances, customers, finding supplies difficult to obtain, may turn to substitute products and the entire market could collapse. It may also be bad practice from a public relations point of view to be seen to be the cause of unemployment among one's competitors.

(i)   In general terms, a market share increase would not be a reliable gauge of an increase in profitability; by the same token, increased turnover in a rapidly expanding market could be coupled with a decline in market share.

(j)   In attempting to increase turnover, a company may indulge in purchases of additional plant and machinery, only to find that the sales expansion is short-lived. Surplus capacity problems could ensue, including having to face heavy fixed costs for maintaining and depreciating idle facilities.

(k)   A turnover increase may indeed result in increased profits, but there may be a disturbing escallation in total capital employed; eg new debtors may be very slow to clear their accounts, or require a very high level of customer service which entails excessive buffer stocks of spares etc.

10 Working Capital Control

The operational trading cycle of a commercial or industrial organisation can involve the spending of money well in advance of the ability to recover it from ultimate customers. At worst, a company's trading cycle can be a long lonely road which it walks almost 'alone' in the sense that few outside sources of temporary finance are available and those which are involved are suspicious and watchful. At best, the time-lag between cost incurrence and recovery in sales can be very short and indebtedness to outside sources of funds very slight. Most companies lie somewhere between these two extremes.

A trading cycle within manufacturing industry involves expenditure on one of the elements of cost (direct material, direct labour, or overheads), and a subsequent delay while the element concerned becomes a part of work in progress, then finished goods and finally a part of cost of sales. A further delay factor then occurs when the goods embodying the original cost outlay are sold on credit, until credit customers decide to settle their accounts. A long time-lag between, say, the purchase of raw materials and the eventual recovery of the cost from customers would represent a real headache for production companies were it not for the fact that the suppliers of the raw materials share the inconvenience of this time lag by offering to delay demands for payment, ie by themselves offering credit.

However, when the time allowed by suppliers of materials, or of services normally constituting part of overheads is less than the time between the date when title to the goods passes and realisation of customers' accounts, a shortfall in availability of funds occurs which has to be made good from other sources, (either within the company from, say, other sales, or from third parties such as banks).

The following example services to illustrate what would be a typical trading cycle for raw materials:

	Average period (days)	Raw Material Trading Cycle
(a)	8	Lying in raw material store
(b)	24	Work-in-progress taking place
(c)	11	Lying in finished goods store as part of finished products
(d)	34	Days' credit to customers after sales point
	77	Total number of days needed before initial material costs are converted to cash through recovery from customers
(e)	31	Less: credit granted from suppliers of raw materials
	46	Length of trading cycle; being time for which finance will need to be found, ie from day 32 until day 77

If anything can be done to shorten the length of (a) to (d), or to extend (e), so much the better. The same type of trading cycle can be built for other elements of cost such as wages and overheads.

Slower Trading Cycles need more Financing

Supposing that a company wishes to raise additional finance for a new trading project. Perhaps they plan usage of additional manufacturing facilities. The amount of additional working capital required can be computed by budgeting the additional cost for a year and multiplying this amount by the number of days in the trading cycle divided by, say, 360 (days in the year, rounded). For example, if the cost of additional materials is expected to be £20,000 in a year, and the trading cycle for materials is 46 days, the sum of £20,000 $\times \frac{46}{360} = £2,555$ would be needed from a source such as a bank; unless, of course, the trading cycle could be reduced in some way by streamlining or through efficiencies. This type of calculation assumes that the liability to pay for materials occurs evenly over the year, for example because of an even flow of raw material deliveries throughout the year. In any event, a 'ponderous' trading cycle can lead to increased finance-servicing costs (interest) and higher administrative costs (storage rents for finished goods and more expensive insurance and security costs, etc). The point at which the company concerned achieves a profit is also likely to be reached less frequently each year (unless the only problem is with slow-paying debtors). Money which has been invested either from within or by outsiders such as banks can 'stick' somewhere along the trading cycle, say at work-in-progress because of poor production scheduling, or at finished goods because of poor selling techniques, or at debtors because of poor credit control.

Distinguishing Cash Flow Forecasts from Cash Budgets

Effective cash budgeting is often evidenced by sound cash flow forecasting systems. Distinctions between a cash budget statement and a cash flow forecast statement are rather intangible. A cash budget format would tend to be in a style preferred by those responsible for what Americans call 'Treasury' work: calling money forward from banks and other finance houses at correct times and in suitable amounts, at economic rates from appropriate sources according to whether it is short-term, middle-term or long-term. The key objectives of those concentrating on the cash budget are to maintain liquidity, and to do so at minimum cost. A cash flow forecast format would often be prepared in styles suitable for showing individual functional managers and managers of specific profit centres the roles which they are playing in generating and spending money. The headings and analysis on cash flow forecasts would harmonise with other accounting reports to such managers, showing costs, profits etc by location and/or division and/or product group.

Frequency of Comparisons of Budgeted and Actual Cash Flows

Cash flow forecasts may be made:

> daily for (say) ten days out
> weekly for (say) six weeks out
> monthly for (say) one year out

The choice of frequency of these 'milestone control' points depends on:

(a) the ability of the company to analyse actual incoming and outgoing cash on a routine basis, to the same detailed levels as shown on forecasts. If accounting expertise and accounting staff time are lacking, it may be impossible to do the job of actual movement analysis every day.
(b) the degree of fluctuation in bank balances from day to day, caused by patterns of debtor receipts and payments to creditors. For example, a cash flow forecasting system showing projections of bank balances at the end of each month for twelve future months could conceal dramatic peaks and troughs in demand for overdraft facilities within particular months.
(c) the degree of credibility attainable when forecasting future events. Forecasts made beyond a certain number of days, weeks or months might be so unreliable as to be at best a waste of time, at worst distinctly misleading.

Distinguishing Cash Flow Forecasts and Funds Flow Statements

There are clear distinctions in contents and format between cash flow forecasts and funds flow statements; the latter are commonly referred to as source and application of funds statements. The professional accounting bodies have issued a Statement of Standard Accounting Practice (SSAP) on this topic and students should become versed in its contents. In particular, source and application of funds statements are a valuable aid to a financial manager or a creditor in evaluating the uses of funds by a firm and in determining how these are financed. Such a statement provides an efficient method for the financial manager to assess the growth of the firm and its resulting financial needs and to determine the best way to finance those needs. Funds flow statements are very useful in planning intermediate and long-term financing.

Additional Financing of Expansion

An example of the computation of additional financing requirements follows: Epsilon Ltd requires financial support for a venture whereby it will increase its annual sales by £100,000. What is the 'peak' amount of additional financing which will be required under the following conditions, assuming that production and selling activity is evenly spread across each year?

(i)   Average length of time during which raw materials are kept in store prior to issue: 2 months

(ii) Length of production cycle (period between issue of materials into factory and completion of goods):   2 months

(iii) Average length of time during which finished goods are in F G store, unsold: $\frac{1}{2}$ month

(iv) Average length of credit granted by suppliers: $1\frac{1}{4}$ months

(v) Credit alowed to customers: $1\frac{1}{2}$ months

(vi) Analysis of Cost plus Profit for additional £100,000 sales:

	%	£
Raw Materials	50	50,000
Direct Labour	30	30,000
Overheads	10	10,000
Profit	10	10,000
	100	£100,000

Suggested solution:

Raw Materials:	Months
Time in R M store	2
Production cycle	2
In F G store	$\frac{1}{2}$
Credit to customers	$1\frac{1}{2}$
	6
Less: credit from suppliers	$1\frac{1}{2}$
Total months to be financed from sources other than suppliers	$4\frac{1}{2}$

Labour   *Months*
    Production cycle   2
    In F G store . . . . $\frac{1}{2}$
    Credit to customers . . . . $1\frac{1}{2}$

    Total months to be financed   4

Overheads
    Production cycle   2
    In F G store . . . . $\frac{1}{2}$
    Credit to customers . . . . $1\frac{1}{2}$

                                                              4

    Less: credit from suppliers . . . . $1\frac{1}{2}$

    Total months to be financed from sources others than suppliers $2\frac{1}{2}$

Maximum Additional Financing

    Raw materials $\frac{4\frac{1}{2}}{12} \times 50,000$ 18,750

    Direct labour $\frac{4}{12} \times 30,000$ 10,000

    Overheads $\frac{2\frac{1}{2}}{12} \times 10,000$ 2,083

                                                              £30,833

After 1.5 months, therefore, Epsilon will need to start paying for raw materials on a routine basis, so that at the end of 6 months, they have paid out £18,750. Thereafter, they will continue to pay for one month's supplies each month, ie £4,166, but will also receive £4,166 each month from customers as part of invoice settlement procedures: so from the start of month 7, incoming cash will be offset against outgoing payments to show a net effect of nil on the bank balance. This levelling off of funding needs from the start of month 7 will apply to each element of cost. Of course customers are likely not only to recompense Epsilon for costs incurred, but also to pay something towards profits. This surplus on inflows may be used to reduce the maximum additional funding of £30,833 or in several other ways such as for further expansion, for machinery purchases or for sales promotional advertising.

Precision in Timing Funding Requirements

As evidenced above, a vital element of cash budgeting involves the timing of peaks and troughs in monetary inflows and outflows, with a best estimate of the maximum aid which could be required from external sources during a future period. In producing such information, cash flow forecasts score a major win over funds flow statements which, if prepared annually, would show only the opening and closing bank balances but reveal nothing of the harrowing liquidity adventures in between.

Ongoing Comparisons of Budgeted and Actual Cash Flows

Another important feature is the routine monitoring of actual cash flow against forecasts. To obtain maximum benefit from such efforts:

(1) the results of trading activities should be clearly displayed, and if there are very diverse activities they should be separated and shown by individual trading activity.

(2) the company's borrowing limits should be clearly stated and compared at each milestone control point with forecast and actual cash balances.

(3) the relevant year's sales should also be displayed in order to provide some base against which to measure particular cash flows.

(4) a full list of assumptions made in forecasting should be attached. Assumptions would be necessary to derive virtually every forecast figure shown, eg as regards sales prices, cost (inflation) trends, customer payment patterns, taxation rates, dates of settlement of creditors' accounts, and discounting policies.

(5) the effects on cash flow of long-term projects should be shown separately, as in such cases income and expenditure would be out of step, and readers of statements would be misled into undue optimism or pessimism.

(6) all cash items should be included.

(7) historical trend information should be shown, eg whereby actual and forecast balances and income and expense details are shown for several preceding periods, as a prelude to study of future period forecasts.

Cash flow information should be as comprehensive as is necessary to show a true and fair view of the state of liquidity of the company concerned. There should not be any 'hidden' stories of impending catastrophe which can only be gleaned by experts after detailed investigation of over-simplified figures. Three examples follow:

Cash Flow No. 1
(£000's)

	Jan.	Feb.	Mar.	Apr.	May	June	July	Aug.	Sept.	Oct.	Nov.	Dec.
Budgeted inflow	1,000	1,000	1,000	1,000	2,000	1,000	1,000	2,000	1,000	1,000	1,500	1,000
Actual inflow	900	850	3,500	840	1,850	700	4,000	1,700	720	750	1,100	2,400
Budgeted outflow	900	1,000	900	1,200	900	1,100	1,000	2,200	1,000	900	1,300	1,100
Actual outflow	950	1,100	900	1,150	1,050	1,300	1,050	2,100	1,100	950	1,400	1,500

The above information is totally inadequate in determining the state of financial and trading health of the company concerned. The 'hidden story' might well be that the company can only continue to function by selling off capital equipment and other fixed assets such as 'so-called' non-essential plant, 'unwanted' subsidiary companies, and 'excess' properties. The point must be made that the company will very quickly run out of such possessions and will then presumably be unable to continue to fund its basic trading expenditures. Clearly the cash flow presentation should have shown separate figures for 'trading operations' and 'capital items'.

Cash Flow No. 2
(£000's)

	Jan.	Feb.	Mar.	Apr.	May	June	July	Aug.	Sept.	Oct.	Nov.	Dec.
Budgeted inflow	1,000	1,050	1,100	1,150	1,200	1,250	1,300	1,300	1,300	1,300	1,400	1,400
Actual inflow	1,000	1.050	1,050	1,100	1,100	1.100	1,050	1,100	1,100	1.150	1,100	1,050
Budgeted outflow	900	900	925	950	975	975	1,000	1,000	1,050	1,050	1,100	1,100
Actual outflow	900	925	925	950	1,000	1,050	1,100	1,100	1,100	1,200	1,250	1,300

Again, the reader has insufficient detail on which to base any judgement. 'Behind the scenes' there could be fierce competition on prices, and customer resistance to price increases. There could also be worrying inflation on the costs front which was going on unchecked by any management action. Some remedy might be found in linking cash flow closely to the amount of invoiced sales (volumes and prices). Costs could be split into fixed and variable elements, and analysed by function into production, selling, distribution and administration, etc. to try to relate possible remedial action to specific individuals.

Cash Flow No. 3
(£000's)

	Jan.	Feb.	Mar.	Apr.	May	June	July	Aug.	Sept.	Oct.	Nov.	Dec.
Budgeted inflow	1,000	1,000	1,100	1,200	1,200	1,300	1,300	1,300	1,200	1,200	1,400	1,400
Actual inflow	1,000	200	900	1,500	300	400	1,400	1,300	600	1,600	1,500	1,400
Budgeted outflow	800	800	850	850	900	1,000	1,050	1,100	1,100	1,100	1,150	1,150
Actual outflow	750	750	800	1,000	800	950	1,000	1,200	1,000	1,000	1,200	1,100

The 'hidden story' in this case could be one of lost sales, where money expected and included in budgeted inflows will never be received. There may well have been too many speculations and gambles during original budgeting exercises. A remedy involves analysing budgeted sales inflow for *risk,* and showing detailed breakdowns, for example, of home versus export sales, and/or new versus old-established and familiar customers. Cash flow statements should be linked closely to invoiced sales turnover achievements, as there is a world of difference between cash shortfalls which will never be made good and those which are caused merely by customers' cheques being delayed in the post.

At any given date, the management accountant may be asked to provide an 'up to date' situation analysis on cash flow. The following framework is relevant:

1 *Cumulative* *(year to date)*	*2* *Current situation* *(most recent period)*	*3* *Future* *situation*
A Budgeted outflow	Budgeted outflow	Budgeted outflow
B Actual outflow	Actual outflow	New forecast
C Actual +/(−) budget	Actual +/(−) budget	Forecast +/(−) budget
D Budgeted inflow	Budgeted inflow	Budgeted inflow
E Actual inflow	Actual inflow	New forecast
F Actual +/(−) budget	Actual +/(−) budget	Forecast +/(−) budget
G Excess/(shortfall) of inflow over outflow – budget	Excess/(shortfall) of inflow over outflow – budget	Excess/(shortfall) of inflow over outflow – budget
H Excess/(shortfall) of inflow over outflow – actual	Excess/(shortfall) of inflow over outflow – actual	Excess/(shortfall) of inflow over outflow – actual

As stated earlier, inflow and outflow totals would require detailed analysis to identify and separate differing risks. For example, outflow might be split between trading expenditure and capital items, with the latter being again divided into (a) essential items which would permit no delay, (b) essential items for which delay could be considered and (c) non-essential items which, in an emergency, could be delayed indefinitely. Inflows could be split between amounts receivable in UK currency and in foreign currencies, with the possibility of exchange rate differences and delays in the latter case.

Elements of Working Capital

Cash is only one of the constituents of working capital. The elements are:

(1)   cash on hand and in the bank, plus easily convertible securities held for short terms

   (2) raw material stocks
   (3) work-in-progress stocks
   (4) finished goods stocks
   (5) debtors
Less
   (6) current liabilities, including trade creditors.

Significance of Working Capital

Working capital represents a margin of safety for short-term creditors. Current assets are likely to yield a higher percentage of their book value on liquidation than do fixed assets. Fixed assets are likely to be more specialised in use and suffer larger declines from book values in a forced liquidation.

The growth in a firm's gross working capital (ie total current assets) may represent a financial problem for a firm, as current assets need to be financed just as do fixed assets. While a company may as a general principle want to streamline its working capital by pruning stockholdings, or reducing the average number of days for which sales accounts remain outstanding, care should be taken not to overlook certain pitfalls. For example, there may be a great deal to commend apparently excessive stock levels: *Ads of high stocks*

   (1) 'The more stock which management carries between stages in the manufacturing – distribution process, the less co-ordination is required to keep the process running smoothly. Contrariwise, if stocks are already being used efficiently, they can be cut only at the expense of greater organisational effort – including greater scheduling effort to keep successive stages in balance, and greater expediting effort to work out of the difficulties which unforeseen disruptions at one point or another may cause in the whole process.'[1]

   (2) The buying department may have been able to take advantage of quantity discounts. As a result, raw material stocks may be temporarily expanded in bulk.

   (3) A reasonable balance of finished goods stock to meet customer demand allows a company flexibility in its production scheduling and in its marketing effort. Production need not be geared directly to sales.

   (4) Given the desire of the marketing department to fulfill orders promptly, large stocks allow efficient servicing of customer demands.

   (5) Customer demand may be unstable enough to warrant high stocks, especially if customer service is of a high standard and the company does not wish to risk stock-out situations.

   (6) Seasonal demand may necessitate ostensibly high stock levels during certain months of the year if the company wishes to stabilise production output levels and avoid lay-offs of labour and consequent problems.

   (7) Stocks may be held in anticipation of an impending price rise.

The general criterion is that stocks may be increased as long as the resulting savings exceed the total cost of holding the added stocks.

In the same vein, a credit control department should have as its dual function the protection of a company's investment in debtors and the promotion of profitable sales. Minimal bad debts should not be the aim; maximum profit should be the aim. In short, pre-occupation with the possibility of bad debts may mean that much needed sales orders are turned down.

Working capital control should not relate only to attempted cut-backs: the principle should be that each £ of working capital must be held for a sound purpose, and control procedures should be aimed at defending this principle.

---

[1]Harvard Business Review.

11 Capital Expenditure Projects

Decisions on capital expenditure can stem from a wide range of needs. For example:

(1) A company may wish to select a suitable machine from a range to expand its production capacity. *expansion*

(2) A machine may be replaced by another which is more or less expensive to operate than its predecessor, but which produces more (or less). *replacement*

(3) A variety of projects may be available which could be supported by funding, but the company concerned cannot afford to support them all. In such cases the criterion for selection may be either a high rate of return on capital employed, with rather a high risk, or a poorer rate of return with less risk.

(4) Escalation of maintenance and repair costs as equipment ages may tip the scales in favour of purchasing new equipment at a substantial cost which will be more than offset by repair cost savings. *new equip*

(5) A company's hand may be forced through new fire, health or safety regulations. *external pressure*

Project Information to be Gathered

Those who are invited to sponsor a capital project should satisfy themselves on the fundamental soundness of any proposals, and the degree of care and skill brought to bear on supporting evidence such as expected lives of new machines and market share to be expected from sales of new product lines. Before a capital expenditure proposal can merit formal acceptance, an impressive array of information should be gathered:

(1) All information necessary to prepare a cash flow forecast, normally discounted back to the date of possible initiation. Anticipated income spread over a project's life is worth less the longer a company has to wait to receive it, and postponement of expenditure carries an advantage over immediate payment. By using discounting techniques, various proposals affecting future income and expense can be compared: future pounds receivable are re-expressed in their present day (year 0) equivalents. For example, if one project (A) involved an immediate payment of £260 (at year 0) and another (B) a payment of £300 in two years' time, discounting could guide management as to which project was preferable, all else being equal. If management considered that any cash held could earn a return of 10% per annum during the 2 years' delay period (or prevent a financing charge of 10% per annum if cash had to be borrowed), a discounting calculation would show that payment of £300 in two years would be about as painful an experience then, as on the spot payment at year 0 of £248. (Discount tables are available in many text books to facilitate such calculations.) Therefore in our example, immediate payment of £260 on project A would be less satisfactory than a delayed payment of £300. As you can imagine, a wide range of assumptions must be made when preparing a cash flow forecast in this way: particularly as regards exact timing of income and expenditure. Careful assessment of timing over what, for some projects, can be many years, can greatly assist in planning financial requirements. Peaks and troughs in monetary supply are highlighted so that appropriate sources of finance can be tapped without embarrassment. Then, assuming liquidity crises can be avoided in this way, relative profitability in cash flow terms of a range of competing projects can be calculated as all monetary sums involved in each are re-expressed as year 0 equivalents. If every sum is brought back to year 0 values, all projects are weighed in a common measure, the year 0 pound.

In what circumstances might it be better for a company to receive, say, £100,000 of income from a project in six years, than £50,000 from another in two years? To attempt an answer the rate which money received early rather than late could earn as soon as received has to be known. Clearly, if there was nothing the company could do with £50,000 for four years (from the end of year 2 until the end of year 6), rejection of the project with the quick return would be preferable. If the company decided to attach a very high value to early procurement of cash rather than the future promise of cash, so that cash held was valued at 18% per annum, they would come to the conclusion that a receipt of £50,000 delayed for 2 years would be worth around $50,000 \times \cdot 718[1] = £35,900$ in year 0 terms: in other words, they would just as readily accept £35,900 at year 0 than £50,000 two years later. Receipt of £100,000 after 6 years, would, using the 18% rate, be equivalent to an immediate (year 0) cash offer of $100,000 \times \cdot 370[1] = £37,000$. Thus the £100,000 project with the slow return would edge out the smaller project, all else being equal.

Another major assumption has to be made about risks involved in potential projects. The longer the likely delay in receiving financial benefit from a planned project, the more vulnerable it can be to erosion through normal business risks such as competitor action, obsolescence or changes in market demand. Previsions of the future are suspect, especially crystal ball gazing beyond three or four years. Some companies, knowing that in their particular situations later cash receipts may be more uncertain than impending income use higher rates for projects involving the former, so that delayed income is penalised during potential project comparisons. Other companies operate in circumstances in which later income is the more certain, and in such cases the above principle may be reversed.

(2) All information necessary to prepare profit forecasts. The timing of incoming and outgoing cash is one thing, pre-planning that someone will be happy to reward the company with operating (sales) income in excess of operating expenditure is something else. A cash flow forecast will include all items of income and expense including capital expenditure, trade-in values and Government grants, but a profit forecast determines whether the project has credibility in terms of gross and net profit percentages; in other words whether there is a potential for self-generating finance from the trading operations which will stem from the project.

(3) Changes to a company's investment base. Clearly, a company's assets growth will involve more than the capital items involved: increased stockholdings of raw materials, work-in-progress and finished goods will result from any expansion, and the total of trade debtors can also be expected to rise, sometimes to embarrassingly high levels if additional credit is the carrot which must be manipulated to attract new sales. Additional profits at (2) above must be measured against the new total investment base, to provide an updated ratio of return on capital employed (ROCE).

(4) Comparisons of the situation with and without a project. Projected cash flow and profit forecasts which simulate project rejection would focus on the effects for example, of possible loss of markets through machine obsolescence or deterioration in customer service levels. A project may be needed not merely to facilitate expansion but also to prevent contraction.

(5) Management authorisation procedures, covering the planning, implementation and post-audit stages. Project evaluation, approval, monitoring and later assessment are best dealt with by small management teams rather than solitary individuals. Responsibility vacuums are always difficult to fill when things go wrong, or when time consuming investigative work is involved. Responsibilities should always be crystal clear for each step from initiation to termination.

(6) Project description and objectives. For example, a company's objective might be to

---

[1] Using discounted cash flow tables

increase its production capacity for satisfying market demand for a single product, or, alternatively to diversify into a wider product range. Another objective might involve the reduction of distribution costs by moving to a location within easy reach of major customers.

(7) Methods of continuing control. When cash flow and profit forecasts are involved, regular milestone control is essential, with actual results being analysed to the same depth and with the same care as forecast results. As soon as regular comparison breaks down, the reliability of future project evaluations is put at risk.

The Discount Rate for Future Income and Expense

On a previous page the fact that a company should discount future income and expense back to year 0 was discussed, but little thought was given to how the actual rate is selected. In considering whether a project should be accepted, the criterion will often be whether the rate of return is at least as good as the return which would be obtained from other projects. Again, the cost of capital invested if a project is accepted may be a vital factor: in this latter case, the company must have an eye to the future. The next project likely to be accepted could possibly be very cheap to finance and pass a far from stringent test on a cost of capital percentage; but it should be required to pass the test of providing a return higher than the *average* cost of the next several increments of capital, some of which may be very expensive.

Thus, while a currently planned project might involve using cash from a debenture issue, interest on which might be 7%, a future project might need to be financed from a merchant bank loan at 13%: it might be very difficult for the company to find a good enough project to surmount the 13% hurdle, but if both the earlier and the later projects were assessed against an average cost, steady growth of the company could be safeguarded.

A Criterion Rate of Return

The situation in which there are enough potential projects on the stocks for a company to set a criterion rate of return which is necessary from any project is illustrated in the following example:

A company has approached you with a view to providing financial assistance for the outright purchase of a new machine costing £20,000. The machine is expected to have a five year life and to produce cost savings of approximately £7,000 per annum during that period. The residual value of the machine after 5 years will be nil. Corporation tax is payable (assume 50%) 12 months after the close of each accounting year. A first year allowance of 100% can be claimed for capital allowances purposes, and there are sufficient profits to absorb all such allowances. The company requires a discounted return of 12% after taxation on all of its capital investments.

Required: prepare a statement showing whether your company should accept the above proposal.

Suggested solution:

DCF Evaluation of Return on Capital (£s)

Year	Cost Saving	Tax @ 50%	Capital Allowances	Tax Saved	Cash Flow	V n/r	Present Value
1	7,000	—	20,000	10,000	17,000	·893	15,181
2	7,000	3,500	—	—	3,500	·797	2,789
3	7,000	3,500	—	—	3,500	·712	2,492
4	7,000	3,500	—	—	3,500	·636	2,226
5	7,000	3,500	—	—	3,500	·567	1,984
6	—	3,500	—	—	−3,500	·507	−1,774
					27,500		22,898

The £22,898 present value of the projected discounted return at 12% is in excess of the cost of £20,000 and therefore it is an acceptable investment. If the cash flow column is added, a net total of £27,500 is obtained. What discounting tells us is that the gradual receipt of £27,500 (net) over six years would be of the same benefit, and provoke the same satisfaction on those occasions, as the receipt of £22,898 NOW. So it is better to go ahead with the proposal in anticipation of £22,898 at 'today's' values, than have no project and £20,000 at 'today's' values. The column V n/r shows the discounting procedure in operation: for example ·893 represents the value of £1 received after a delay of 1 year, when immediate receipt of the £1 could have provided a return for the year of 12%.

Whether to Replace or Repair Plant

Manufacturing companies can be faced with a decision as to whether to replace certain items of plant and machinery or to carry out extensive repairs which would increase their working lives. A balanced decision as to whether or not to replace existing plant and machinery depends on a comparison of costs of the alternatives. There are many elements of cost which must be included in this comparison, apart from the more obvious ones such as preventive maintenance and plant repairs. For example, the quality of service rendered by an ageing machine may begin to fall, in which case it is necessary to estimate the losses in which this may involve the company. 'There may be increased wastage of materials, a fall in the rate of production, and possibly some direct loss of revenue or customer goodwill due to relatively inferior products. All of these should be estimated for each year the asset is kept in production'[1]. The staff of the production director can be of assistance in scheduling the above elements of cost which can be classified as 'operating costs'.

For the purposes of cost comparison, the cost of the capital outlay for new plant must be included with operating costs. Taxation allowances may have a significant bearing on asset valuation.

It is clear from the above that the extension of the life of machinery through repairs could certainly be to the disadvantage of the company even if the cost of the repair in question was small, as the machines could continue in use at well below a desirable performance level.

To the costs of possible new machinery must be added the less obvious elements such as employee re-training, and dismantling of old equipment and construction foundations for the new.

In assessing the alternatives of whether to retain or replace machinery, there is also the possible cost of a 'lost opportunity' in retaining an existing machine and depriving the company of the productivity improvement derived from new machinery. This improvement can be measured by comparing the performance of the existing machinery under conditions of normal efficiency with that of the new machinery under such conditions. To make this comparison possible the production director must make himself thoroughly familiar with the capabilities of the proposed machinery under conditions similar to those prevailing in the company.

The production director can be of great assistance in evaluating certain other information which is likely to be needed in making a decision, viz:

(1) the reliability of asset lives,
(2) the significance, and degree of risk, of obsolescence,
(3) the significance of production bottlenecks which could be cleared by new machinery, or created by new machinery in other production departments which would be unable to cope with additional intake from re-equipped departments.

---

[1] Merrett & Sykes, 'The Finance and Analysis of Capital Projects'.

The production director should also participate in the assessment of as wide a range of options as possible, eg whether or not to buy machines with expanded capacity, whether to obtain one large machine to two smaller ones at different sites, or whether to take an opportunity to sub-contract the production work perhaps in view of a rapidly declining product life-span.

One of the major influences in determining asset lives is the life-span of the end products ultimately marketed by the company and which the equipment in question helps to produce. If the remaining life span of the end-products is assessed as short, the viability of new equipment must be questioned, unless the production director can give assurances that the equipment could be converted at acceptable cost to alternative uses.

A major financial consideration of which the production director should be aware, would be the purchasing options open to the company, eg hire purchase, outright purchase, rental or lease, etc.

Replacement of plant usually involves the company in long-term commitment. Further repairs to existing plant can offer a 'breathing space' until the company is reasonably certain that there will be a continuing demand for the end-products concerned.

Regional development, EEC and local authority grants should be evaluated, especially if these are not being offered on an indefinite basis.

Uniform Procedures for Submitting Capital Expenditure Requests

In some companies it may be possible to adopt a uniform procedure for the submission of requests for authorisation of capital expenditure, particularly if there is already a continuous need for the authorising parties eg the Board, to amplify or summarise individual requests, and to adapt information into a common style and format for decision making; standardisation can offer a potential solution to the time-wasting and difficulty involved.

It is felt that such a solution could be feasible even if the company concerned were diversified, and projects being appraised related to different industries and/or functions. Potential projects could be judged against common criteria and yardsticks, eg each categorised as one of the following: replacement, expansion, cost saving, development, or safety/hygiene. A view would be taken on whether management support could be successfully canvassed on the grounds that the proposals regarding uniformity would be intended to save enquiry, re-drafting and discussion time, and would also go a long way towards ensuring that no relevant factors were overlooked in judging particular products. A standardised range of information on each project would present the danger of overlooking 'special situations' and there would be a continuing need to measure and evaluate projects against several yardsticks rather than a single yardstick of, say, profitabilty.

There would be some advantage in standardisation if authorisation levels could also be 'standardised', say at certain monetary levels, according to project category, eg all expansions over £10,000 might require authorisation at Board level while all replacements over £15,000 might require similar authorisation.

Standardisation of submission procedures would help to ensure optimum background investigation by management proposers, in line with written instructional manuals; however if such preparatory work was already satisfactory one of the benefits of standardisation would be lost. An optimum level for certain managers would often be well *below* superceded levels: excess detail would be eliminated.

The standardised procedures would need the support of all levels of management, as they could be applied by divisional/functional management when selecting an ultimate choice of project for approval at the next authorisation stage from a range of possibilities.

Prior agreement by the Board that the level of expenditure at which Board authorisation was required could be raised after a trial period, would confirm substantial time savings for higher management levels. A trustworthy standardised system could in effect result in a general raising of authorisation levels with periodic test-checks to confirm that internal control procedures were effective.

Investigations would confirm whether it would be possible, in due course, to monitor actual against forecast results for each project, in the standard format. A major benefit of standardisation would be the regular presentation of comparative, 'post-audit' information assessing in effect whether management judgment had been sound.

The essential overall factor would be the extent and persistence of demand for uniform procedures, and the general level of management support. It would also be essential to study any previous attempts to implement such procedures, and to assess any reasons for failure.

Acid Tests before Accepting Proposals

Growing companies need to harness the enthusiasm of management responsible for optimistic capital projects and ensure that evaluations are particularly searching. For example, a proposal might be put forward to build a factory extension in the belief, sincerely held, that market demand was about to exceed the company's ability to produce. Factors to be considered in this promising situation would be:

(1) The levels of support for the proposal, including full details of sponsors. A careful appraisal would be made of the reliability of the background information which supported the proposal, eg sales forecasts. A view would be taken as to whether the degree of risk could be reliably assessed.

(2) The long-term strategy of the company. Clarification would be needed that such an expansion was in harmony with the general plans for growth. Alternative plans could include the opening of additional sites rather than single site expansion.

(3) Availability of space. Apart from this obvious but vital factor, planning permission would be needed.

(4) The products involved in the expansion. Product life assessments would be needed; the longer-term reliability of the market, possible competitor action, and whether the extension could in fact be built in time to capture and retain an expanded market would all require confirmation.

(5) External issues, such as the state of the economy, government policies and pressures, and the opportunities and threats emanating from the environment of the company's operations.

(6) Efficiency of present usage of capacity. Full consideration would be given to the possibility of streamlining within existing capacity parameters. Double or treble shift working, and productivity agreements could economically increase output without requiring expansion of facilities.

(7) Options. These would include sub-contracting at economic rates, shedding certain less profitable products, and opening another site elsewhere. The question of sub-contracting would involve detailed investigation into potential sub-contractors' ability to meet product quality and size specifications and potential deadlines, and their general performance records in the past on similar work.

(8) Availability of funds. Analysis of possible sources with interest rates and repayment terms would reveal whether plans were feasible. The possibility of obtaining Government grants or government agency grants/loans would be investigated.

(9) Limiting factors. There would be an assessment of labour and raw material availability, and any other resources which might prove to be limiting factors.

(10) Disruption factors. Badly handled, extensions could disrupt production and lose customer goodwill, so that when the new capacity became available, order book entries might be in decline.

(11) Effects on product quality. It could prove difficult for old and new machinery to make identical products. The age and condition of existing machinery would be considered, and

whether for one reason or another, the extension would result at an early date in the re-equipping of the older part of the factory site.

(12) Value of available information on which to take a decision. An ultimate decision would need the preparation of cash flow forecasts to assess profitability, financing requirements and risk, including as a major aspect the degree of dependence upon greatly increased sales in order to survive.

(13) Authorisation procedures. Clarification would be needed that management would be prepared to adhere to strict authorisation procedures regarding all expenditure involved.

Post-audit

A vital step in the management of a capital budget is the 'post-completion audit'. For example, after a new factory extension started production, just on schedule, sales of the new product brand involved might well 'exceed expectations', but if the extension cost was a bombshell, production costs higher than expected, and sales levels liable to fall away after the initial euphoria produced by special publicity and promotion schemes, post-audit techniques would identify the problems and, equally important, help management not to repeat mistakes.

Attention is drawn to unsuccessful projects; whatever additional action is needed to raise the company to the giddy heights of planned performance is taken. Audits of this kind adhere to the principle that the best method of achieving conscientious forecasting for the future is to take a long, lingering look at earlier forecasts and ask whether they have been met, or are being met. Management's decision making skills are sharpened by testing earlier decisions for soundness.

Post-audit work should be performed by personnel who have a good general knowledge of the wider implications of the project, (marketing, technical, financial, etc). Such personnel should be independent of the project team responsible for advocating the project. Factors to be covered would include:

(1) whether the promised benefits were being received;
(2) whether any remedial action was necessary;
(3) the speed with which planned benefits were being derived;
(4) whether there were any unforeseen installation costs or operation costs;
(5) whether there was greater than anticipated training time.

However even with extensive and sophisticated post-audit techniques, sponsors of new capital projects may be let off the hook because their harrowing forecasts of impending misfortunes which would befall *without* their projects can never be tested in retrospect. 'If we don't replace this machine, it will start to break down every week.' Should the machine be replaced, it is usually scrapped, and whether it would in fact have had such a poor performance becomes pure conjecture. A difficult objective of post-audit reviews is to motivate management into putting as much care and skill into projecting and evaluating performance in the company with the old machinery should it be given a further lease of life, as they would wish to inject in assessing the capabilities of possible new machinery. A more easily attainable objective of post-audit is to compare the actual performance of new machinery against the anticipated performance on which the project was 'sold'.

Glossary of Terms and Expressions Used

Administration Overhead: 'The sum of those costs of general management, and of secretarial, accounting and administrative services, which cannot be directly related to the production, marketing, research or development functions of the enterprise' (ICMA 'Terminology').

Accounting Code: is a series of alphabetical and/or numerical symbols, each of which represents a descriptive title in a cost, income, asset, liability or statistical classification.

Absorption of Overheads: can also be termed 'overhead recovery', and is the process of assigning overhead to products or saleable services by means of overhead recovery rates. Computation of a specific rate to be charged is based on dividing the total overhead to be absorbed in a department or other entity by the number of units of activity in that location to obtain a recovery rate per unit of activity. Activity is expressed as direct labour hours, machine hours, raw material pounds (value) direct labour pounds (value) or some other similar measure which reflects the actual cause of overhead costs.

Absorption Costing: the practice of applying fixed factory (and sometimes administration) overhead to goods (or services) produced. In due course, selling costs may also be attributed to and absorbed by specific products or services at time of sale, at a unit absorption rate intended to spread equitable cost portions to individual units, thus deriving as full a cost per product unit as possible.

Activity: the degree to which the capacity of an organisation has been exploited, usually expressed as a number of units of output (for production activity) or sales (for selling activity). It is essential when answering examination questions involving production or selling activity (or both) to define the *measure* of that activity (eg steel blades, jars of jam, castings, passenger-miles), and then to identify the actual level of that activity which has been achieved (eg 950 steel blades produced).

Allocation of Overheads: involves 'the allotment of whole items of cost to cost centres or cost units' (ICMA 'Terminology'). It is assumed that each item of cost is separately identifiable with one such department or cost centre. An example would be the charging of a supervisor's salary from a payroll analysis to a specific cost centre where he spent all of his chargeable time.

Apportionment of Costs: 'The allotment to two or more cost centres of proportions of common items of cost on the estimated basis of benefit received' (ICMA 'Terminology'). Some equitable arithmetical fractions must be found to represent the incidence of these items at the places where they are incurred. For example, local authority rates may be apportioned to cost centres on the basis of floor area.

Budgets: 'Financial and/or quantitative statements, prepared and approved prior to a defined period of time, of the policy to be pursued during that period for the purpose of attaining a given objective. They may include income, expenditure and the employment of capital' (ICMA 'Terminology').

Business Resources: in this context taken to mean manpower, money, materials, machinery, building space, 'know-how' and information.

Budgetary Control: 'The establishment of budgets relating the responsibilities of executives to the requirements of a policy, and the continuous comparison of actual with budgeted results, either to secure by individual action the objective of that policy or to provide a basis for its revision' (ICMA 'Terminology').

Break-even Point: the selling activity level at which the sales turnover exactly equals the sum of the variable costs and the fixed costs incurred, so that neither a profit nor a loss is incurred.

Contribution: the difference between the selling price of a product, process or job and its marginal cost.

Contribution Margin Ratio: that part of each pound of sales which can be set aside, after variable costs have been paid, to help to recover fixed costs and to boost profits.

100

Control Accounts: are nominal (or general) ledger accounts which are maintained for stock accounts and debtors' and creditors' accounts, and which reflect the total situations to be found in detailed accounts within subsidiary ledgers. The use of the word 'control' implies that a subsidiary ledger is maintained, detailing separate subsidiary ledger accounts for each job, process, product, raw material or finished goods part etc. The balance of a control account should always equal the total of the balances on the individual accounts in the subsidiary ledger.

Cost Centre: the full title is 'cost collection centre'. It is an area of responsibility for which costs may be collected to promote business objectives, eg the spreading of manufacturing costs over units of production passing through a particular centre. Cost centres are used as points of cost control, where actual and expected costs are compared by specific managers.

Cost Control: procedures whereby actual costs incurred at actual production and selling activities are compared on an ongoing basis against the costs which, according to pre-determined calculations, ought to have been incurred at such (actual) levels. Clearly original, budgeted cost levels have to be flexed or adjusted to bring expense entitlement levels into line with actual activities.

Cost of Sales: this may be 'the total cost of production, marketing, general administration and research and development, attributable to the products or services sold during a specified accounting period' (ICMA 'Terminology') or it may relate only to the production cost of sales, or to the production and administration cost of sales, depending on the level of profit assessment ('gross', 'net', etc) required. In any event, 'COST OF SALES' should have an appropriate prefix, eg 'Total Cost of Sales' or 'Production Cost of Sales'.

Capacity: hours available for possible application to production effort. Capacity may be a theoretical maximum (eg 7 days × 24 hours per day = 168 hours) or a practical capacity (eg (say) 5 days × 8 hours per day = 40 hours). Capacity can also be expressed in production unit terms, eg '1,000 tonnes per week'.

Capacity Ratio: 'The actual number of direct working hours charged (in an accounting period) divided by or expressed as a percentage of the budgeted number of standard hours. A ratio higher than 100% indicates that more hours were utilised in practice that were earmarked (booked in advance), so that when direct operatives exploit these actual hours used at an efficiency of at least 100% (one hour's worth of output from one hour's effort), the production unit concerned will produce an output level in excess of budget.

Direct Material: raw material which, via invoices or stores requisition slips or other basic documentation, can be charged to specific products, jobs or processes without the need for some arbitrary re-apportionment, or guess-work as to how a total charge for that material can best be split over more than one product. Consumables such as paint and lubricating oil for manufacturing machinery are not regarded as direct materials when they can only be directly charged to departments or cost centres and then spread on some arbitrary basis over a number of products through inclusion in overhead recovery procedures.

Direct Labour: all labour which is chargeable by means of time sheets etc to specific products, processes or jobs.

Downtime: time which is a part of the capacity of a manufacturing unit but during which production has ceased, either on a planned or unexpected basis. Budgeted downtime may be expressed as a percentage either of total capacity or of practical capacity. It may sometimes represent the difference between practical capacity (in hours) and activity (in hours).

Direct Labour Efficiency Variance: that part of a total variance, (between actual profit and the budgeted profit at actual output levels), which is brought about by a difference between actual direct hours charged and the number of hours which *ought* to have been charged (according to standards) at the actual production level. The difference is evaluated at the standard rate per direct labour hour.

Direct Material Usage Variance: that part of a total variance (see **Direct Labour Efficiency Variance**) which is brought about by a difference between the quantity of direct materials actually used at the actual production level and the quantity which ought to have been used (according to standards) at that level. The difference is evaluated at the standard unit purchase price of the materials concerned.

Direct Material Price Variance: better practice involves evaluating the difference between actual quantity purchased at standard buying prices and actual quantity purchased at actual prices. This variance is again a part of the total profit variance referred to previously.

Direct Labour Rate Variance: that part of a total variance which is brought about by using actual hourly wage rates which differ from standard rates. The difference is evaluated using the actual direct labour hours worked.

101

Direct Labour Cost Variance: the total financial impact on the budgeted profit due at the actual production level, which is brought about by having to pay a different amount for direct wages than was expected (according to standards) at that level. This variance can often be analysed into rate and efficiency variances.

Direct Material Cost Variance: the total financial impact on the budgeted profit due at the actual production level, which is brought about by having to use a different quantity of raw materials at different prices from standard. This variance can often be analysed into the usage and price variances.

Expense Classifications: categories of cost which are used to facilitate the analysis of total expenditure into manageable and meaningful elements, so that deviations between actual and budgeted costs become more significant and can bring about management action. Examples: salaries; training costs; recruitment costs; travelling expenses.

Fixed Costs: those costs the total of which does not fluctuate with movements in activity levels: fixed production costs, for example, do not change with production level changes, and fixed selling costs are likewise insensitive to changes in sales activity. It must be remembered that fixed costs may remain fixed only within certain ranges of activity. For example, after a certain level of production has been reached, new machinery may be involved which necessitates additional fixed costs such as preventive maintenance and insurance.

Fixed Production Overhead Volume Variance: the extent to which budgeted fixed expenditure has been over- or under-absorbed (recovered) by units of production. The standard fixed cost recovery rate is mutiplied by the excess of actual units over budgeted units or by the shortfall if actual production is less. This variance provides part of the explanation as to why actual profit is greater/less than the originally budgeted profit.

Fixed Production Overhead Expenditure Variance: the difference between the budgeted fixed production overhead cost and the actual cost for an accounting period. This variance forms part of the total profit variance already mentioned.

Fixed Production Overhead Variance: the sum total of the fixed production overhead expenditure variance and the fixed production overhead volume variance.

Flexible Budget: a budget which, through recognition of the difference in behaviour between fixed and variable costs as activity levels fluctuate, can be revised so that the actual costs at any particular activity level can be properly compared with the costs which should have been incurred at that actual activity level.

Indirect Costs: costs which cannot be traced directly to specific products, jobs or processes. The term may also be used to describe costs which cannot be traced directly to a particular cost centre; for example, a share of a works canteen total deficit would be an indirect cost to particular manufacturing cost centres whose employees used the canteen. At product level, the salary of a works foreman who did not charge his time to specific products would be an indirect cost to be included in product costs as part of overheads.

Limiting Factor: 'The factor which, at a particular time, or over a period, will limit the activities of an undertaking. The limiting factor is usually the level of demand for the products or services of the undertaking, but it could be a shortage of one of the productive resources, eg skilled labour or raw material . . .' (ICMA 'Terminology').

Manufacturing (or Production) Cost Centre: a cost centre which adds tangible value to a saleable product. Production activity entering such a cost centre should be capable of assessment in some definable measure, eg unpainted vehicles, as should production leaving the cost centre, eg painted vehicles.

Marginal Cost: the total of the variable costs, normally direct materials, direct labour and variable overheads, attributable either to one product unit or to a total of units. This cost amounts to the chargeable total which will arise directly as a result of making a particular unit or units, and which would be avoided if the unit or units were not made.

Margin of Safety: that part of a total sales turnover either achieved or planned, which could be eliminated so that the company concerned fell back to a sales level at which it made neither a profit nor a loss (break-even point).

Production Volume Ratio: the relationship between budgeted output and actual output achieved, expressed as a percentage. When actual output exceeds budgeted output the ratio will be greater than 100%, and therefore favourable. Unless this ratio is to be analysed further, it is not necessary to convert budgeted and actual output to standard hours.

Productivity (or Efficiency) Ratio: the relationship between actual direct hours worked and standard hours' worth of output achieved. If the output hours exceed actual hours, the ratio will be greater than 100%, and therefore favourable.

Product Cost: the total of those categories of cost which form part of stock valuation. Such costs can therefore be removed from the time period in which they were actually incurred, provided there is a closing stock of the product concerned which is expected to be saleable for at least the total of those costs, ie provided the costs are realisable in due course.

Prime Cost: the total cost of direct materials, wages and expenses. The term normally includes only production costs.

Profit Centre: see page 43.

Raw Material Variance: see **Direct Material Variances**

Sales Volume Variance: the difference between an originally budgeted profit and an actual profit which is caused by selling more or fewer units than budgeted. The physical quantity difference is multiplied by the standard profit per unit, except when marginal costing is used, when the standard contribution per unit is used.

Sales Price Variance: that part of a total variance between actual profit and what that profit should have been (according to standards) at that actual activity level, which is brought about by changing unit selling prices from standard to actual. The actual sales quantity is multiplied by the difference between the actual and standard selling prices.

Scrap Ratio: that proportion of total production output which fails to reach the finished goods stock stage or the next production department. The total of the scrap and production yield ratios should be 100%.

Trading Cycle: for any particular category of cost such as direct materials is the length of time for which the cost of that element must be financed prior to cash being received from the customers concerned. The gross length of a trading cycle is often reduced by the amount of credit time allowed by suppliers. Thus a trading cycle represents the time beyond supplier credit terms, for which finance must be found either from third parties, or from within the finances or other operations of the organisation.

Standard Cost: 'A carefully predetermined cost that should be attained; usually expressed per unit'. (C. T. Horngren; 'Cost Accounting, A Managerial Emphasis', 3rd Edition.)

Service Department (or Cost Centre): is one which does not directly handle saleable commodities in the sense of adding any tangible value. Examples are the power-house, canteen, first aid department, works personnel department.

Variable Costs: those categories of cost which vary in total with changes in activity levels, eg direct materials.

Variance: a deviation of actual results from expected or budgeted results: a specific variance arises from comparing actual costs of a particular category with standard cost, or actual sales with budgeted sales.

Yield Ratio: may either by the relationship of good output weight of saleable commodity to the weight of input entering a process (expressed as a percentage), or the proportion (as a percentage) of total production (in units) which passes inspection and proceeds to finished goods account in the nominal ledger as saleable, or to the next production department.

Yield Variance: this variance may be that part of a DIRECT MATERIAL USAGE VARIANCE which is caused by using excess or short measure of input bulk of mixed ingredients in a manufacturing process (as compared with standard total bulk allowed for the given production activity level). However when there is only one raw material ingredient, the DIRECT MATERIAL YIELD VARIANCE is the same as the DIRECT MATERIAL USAGE VARIANCE, in which case the latter expression is preferred. Again, this variance may be the standard output cost of those finished units which were unexpectedly scrapped (unfavourable variance), or of those which were expected to be scrapped from the total activity level achieved, but which survived (favourable variance).